IT'S NEVER TOO LATE TO SLEEP TRAIN

The Low-Stress Way
to High-Quality Sleep for
Babies, Kids and Parents

DR CRAIG CANAPARI

yellow
kite

First published in Great Britain in 2019 by Yellow Kite
An Imprint of Hodder & Stoughton
An Hachette UK company

First published in the United States of America in 2019 by Rodale Books,
An imprint of the Crown Publishing Group

This paperback edition published in 2021

1

A CIP catalogue record for this title is available from the British Library

Paperback ISBN 978 1 529 35548 2

Printed and bound in Great Britain by Clays Ltd, Elcograf S.p.A.

Hodder & Stoughton policy is to use papers that are natural, renewable and recyclable products and made from wood grown in sustainable forests. The logging and manufacturing processes are expected to conform to the environmental regulations of the country of origin.

Yellow Kite
Hodder & Stoughton Ltd
Carmelite House
50 Victoria Embankment
London EC4Y 0DZ

www.yellowkitebooks.co.uk

To Jeanna, Charlie, and Teddy—
you're the reason I get out of bed in the morning.
In the case of Teddy, often literally.

CONTENTS

IT'S NEVER TOO LATE TO SLEEP TRAIN

INTRODUCTION

JANE WAS CRYING in my office. I passed her a box of tissues. "I can't remember the last time I've had a good night of sleep," she told me, sniffling.

She was a well-dressed woman in her late thirties. Her husband, who had come straight from his job at the hospital, looked down at his well-worn clogs. Nathan, their thirteen-month-old boy, quietly sat in his mother's lap, playing with her purse straps.

"Everything was going pretty well for the first five months, but then we went on a trip," Jane explained. "He wouldn't go to sleep on his own, so I nursed him to sleep and put him down between us. Since then, Nathan refuses to go to sleep without me."

"Tell me about a typical night in your home," I asked.

"We have dinner around 6:00 p.m., then Nathan has a bath. We go to his room and read some stories. Then I need to lie down with him in our bed to nurse him to sleep. If I'm lucky, I can get up for a few hours, but sometimes I just fall asleep. After 11:00 p.m. he wakes me up to feed every few hours. Then he's up at 5:00 a.m."

"What have you tried to address this?"

"We tried the cry-it-out method, but he cried until he threw up, so we stopped."

"What are you most worried about?"

"Well, I'm going back to work full-time, and I'm really worried I won't be able to function. This has been really hard on my marriage as well. My husband usually goes and sleeps in the other room. More than anything, though, *I'm worried I've ruined my son's sleep.*"

I'VE BEEN IN sleep medicine for a decade and direct the Yale Pediatric Sleep Center in New Haven, Connecticut. In my practice, I see people from all walks of life who struggle with the sleep of their children—single parents and married couples, doctors, construction workers, waiters, hedge fund managers, and car dealers. These parents have a few things in common: They love their children and want what is best for them. They are exhausted. And they don't know what to do about it.

If you've picked up this book, I'm guessing that you are in a similar position. Perhaps Jane's story is similar to your own. Or maybe you have a five-year-old who comes into your room ten times a night. Or maybe your three-year-old has a mega-tantrum every night when it's time to brush her teeth and go to her bedroom.

If your child isn't sleeping well at night, this book is for you.

This book has one goal: getting your child to fall asleep, stay asleep, and wake up happy in the morning. And that means that you can fall asleep, stay asleep, and wake up happy in the morning.

This book is designed to be useful for even the most tired parent. I encourage you to read it front to back, but each chapter will begin with a clear description of its contents. If, say, your child sleeps in his own room and does not nurse, you can skip the parts aimed at parents who need to wean a nursing toddler who won't sleep in his own room.

Good sleep is the foundation of health and success for everyone in your family. It is necessary for growth, health, safety, and *happiness*.

Bad Sleep Sucks

Sleep problems are *incredibly* common in children. More than a quarter of parents will discuss sleep issues with their child's pediatrician. This is only the tip of the iceberg, as parents tend to underreport behavioral issues, out of a misguided impression that acknowledging them reflects failure as parents. Another survey of parents of young children said that a whopping 90 percent of parents would change something about their child's sleep. And not only are sleep problems common, but the consequences of them can be severe.

Sleep debt is cumulative. That means the cost to your mood and attention increases the longer your sleep is disrupted. It's hard enough to balance home and work when you feel energized and awesome. Trying to do it when you're addled by lack of sleep is a serious challenge. No wonder being a sleep perfectionist has become so trendy. According to a recent article in the *New York Times*, "sleep is the new status symbol." Executives who once bragged about how little sleep they need now brag about how much they get every night. Expensive sleep gadgets, gear, and consultants are all the rage.

But, as the *Times* article confirmed, sleep is a serious health issue—and a serious public health issue, too. The average grown-up (say, you or me) who misses just two hours of sleep two nights in a row suffers effects similar to those of someone was has missed a full night of sleep. And driving tired can be as dangerous as driving drunk. That's why many states now have drowsy-driving laws that consider sleep-deprived drivers to be legally impaired. Sleep deprivation is also responsible for a wide range of serious health problems, including depression.

Your children may fare a little bit better after a sleepless night than you do. They can always catch a short nap here and there, in the car or stroller. Still, those odd intervals of sleep don't yield the same benefits as a good night's sleep. Research shows that tired kids have a hard time regulating their behavior and retaining information. Small children who are sleep deprived aren't likely to nod off in the sandbox. They are much more likely to be hyperactive, to struggle with peers, and to be obese. And they are more likely to experience sleep problems throughout childhood and adolescence, perhaps even into adulthood (surveys of adults with insomnia suggest that sleep problems commonly start in childhood). A study from Australia of more than two thousand children showed that children who were able to sleep independently through the night by age five had a significant advantage over their peers in terms of emotional regulation.

Many of the families I see in my practice have grappled with significant sleep deprivation for years. Their child may wake up punishingly early, or demand five feedings per night. He may require such long stretches of his parents' evening to get to sleep that they have practically no time left for anything else—paying the bills, relaxing, sharing intimacy, or combing through the dizzying array of sleep advice. The parents who come to the Yale Pediatric Sleep Center are there, first and foremost, because they are worried about their child's sleep. But they are worried too about their own ability to keep going.

I know how it feels, because I've been there.

I was a pediatric resident at Massachusetts General Hospital in Boston back in the dark ages before there were work hour regulations. Until 2003, doctors in training weren't guaranteed any uninterrupted rest during their shifts. I worked thirty-six hours at a stretch, and if I was lucky, I'd catch a few hours of sleep in the on-call rooms, interrupted by only a few pages. At the end of my shift, I drove home carefully, doing my best to stay alert on the road. I collapsed on the couch as soon as I arrived and spent my few waking hours miserable and irritable. I loved my patients and my work, but basically, I was in a bad mood for three years.

Medical residents have infamously grueling schedules. But not even those three long years of training prepared me for the extreme sleep deprivation that is parenthood. The big difference: *parents don't get a break*. When I was a resident, I had at least two to three nights off before going back to the hospital for my next overnight shift. Many parents don't have *any* uninterrupted nights of sleep in their foreseeable future. Unlike residents, most parents don't have a small army of experts on-site to consult whenever they're unsure what to do.

My kids are in elementary school now and they're both great sleepers compared to some of my friends' and my patients' kids— and it can still be terrible. Here's a garden-variety example: One week not long ago, my nine-year-old somehow got croup (four years past the typical age) plus an ear infection. My six-year-old got a stomach bug. These are all minor afflictions. But combined with packed work schedules and an important deadline, it added up to a train wreck of a week for the whole family. At least one child woke up a couple of times per night, needing clean sheets, ibuprofen, or a lost teddy bear. The boys would repeatedly creep into our bed, and we would repeatedly return them. One night I would escape to the guest room, and the next night my wife would; it was our half-assed attempt at taking shifts. When I flunked the boys' breakfast one morning ("Too much butter!"), my older son asked me where Mommy was. The answer: hiding under a duvet in the guest room.

I love my kids more than I can say. But on those sleepless days, I was definitely not the parent I aspire to be. I was irritable with my kids and pretty much everyone else. I ate poorly. (Research confirms that short or fragmented sleep is associated with increased craving for sugary foods.) I didn't exercise. I drank (a lot) more coffee than usual so that I wouldn't fall asleep on my long daily commutes home from the clinic. And this disruption lasted only a few days; for many of the families I see, this has been a way of life for years.

Parents are often racked with guilt about sleep issues. Like Jane, they worry that they have ruined their child's sleep. Or, since their child is out of infancy, they think they have somehow missed a magical window to improve their child's sleep and are now stuck with it until their child graduates from high school. (It's easy to think in this catastrophic manner when you are exhausted.)

Here's the thing: *it doesn't have to be this way*. Your child can sleep better, and so can you. You're not a monster for desiring this. There's a saying that you are only as happy as your least happy child. I would turn this on its head and say that your child is only as happy as her least happy parent. If you are at your wits' end from exhaustion and sleep deprivation, you owe it to yourself, your partner, and your child to fix it.

Don't worry about what has come before. Focus on what you can control now. But before we talk about *how* to make a change, let's talk about *why*.

What Can Better Sleep Do for You?

Why do you want to make a change? I know you want your child to sleep better, and to sleep better yourself. I won't lie to you—this process can be challenging at times. But the rewards can be great. Imagine if:

- Your child goes to bed easily and wakes up playful and in a great mood at the same time every day.
- Bedtime is a lovely time that you share with your child, starting with calming activities, proceeding to cuddles, and ending when you kiss your child good night and leave the room.
- You and your partner have some time together in the evening to do activities you enjoy, *without* your kids.
- You can leave your child with a family member or babysitter without worrying about a huge freak-out, and with confidence that your child will be asleep when you get home.
- You wake up in the morning feeling *awesome*.

I'm going to help you get there. First, write down three concrete benefits that you imagine achieving from reading this book. Not just "Sleep better" but "Sleep better so I can get in my morning run more often and maybe run that half marathon I've been meaning to do." Just the act of writing these things down will help you succeed. When sleep training gets hard—and it likely will get harder before it gets better—remembering *why* you are doing it can help you keep going.

Why Me? Why This Book?

There are lots of sleep books out there. As a parent and a sleep physician, I have learned a lot from many of them. Why write another one?

As director of the Yale Pediatric Sleep Center and a practicing physician, I see hundreds of families a year with struggles just like yours. Many of them face severe or seemingly intractable sleep issues that may have gone on for months or years. This book addresses the challenges these families face. But I know that there are many other families out there who crave solutions. Maybe their problems are intermittent; maybe they don't have access to a sleep specialist. But they still need support.

I've had over 2.5 million visits to my website, drcraigcanapari .com, since I started it in 2012. Clearly, people are hungry for an easier approach to dealing with sleep problems in their family. Life has changed since Dr. Richard Ferber and Dr. Marc Weissbluth wrote their books in the 1980s. It is far less common now to have a parent at home full-time, and the demands of dual workplace routines in our 24/7 world make sleep schedules less flexible and time scarcer than ever. Social media is stressing us all out—watching the carefully curated Instagrams of our friends makes us feel inadequate. Single-parent families are more common, too, and they face new challenges that call for new solutions. To state the obvious, the sleep stakes are even higher when you're the only caretaker on duty and you need to be at your desk at 8:00 a.m. sharp. Blended families can complicate sleep training as well. Choosing a consistent sleep-training method that works for all parties involved may resemble a negotiated settlement. Studies also show that children in urban settings tend to have worse sleep—and that sleep is significantly affected by socioeconomic status.

My approach is simple, customizable, and easy to understand. Based on my extensive experience in clinics at Harvard and Yale, and interacting with thousands of parents who have left comments on my website and emailed me, I've created a streamlined approach that I think will help parents of children from six months of age through elementary school.

I had a few specific groups of families in mind when I wrote this book:

- Families in crisis, who need to fix their child's sleep problem as quickly as possible.
- Parents of older children, who often are trying to apply infant sleep techniques (such as extinction, sometimes known as cry-it-out or CIO) without success. Most conventional sleep-training advice will not be effective for older children. (Don't worry, we'll talk about infants as well.) Whether your child is six months or six years old, you will find help here.
- Busy parents who want a simple pathway, with clear action items and troubleshooting for a wide range of issues, that also has the flexibility to meet their own particular needs.

The goal of this book is to help children fall asleep and stay asleep without help. If parents follow the steps in this book, they will get to this goal.

What's the magic?

We're going to hack the habit loop, that powerful driver of many of our fundamental behaviors, including sleep. The habit loop is a cycle of behavior that happens over and over without conscious thought on our part, and it underlies many of the repetitive battles we have with our children over sleep. We'll review it in detail in Chapter 2. What's more, we're going to change your child's repetitive, troublesome actions by making changes in your own behavior—so that you don't have to resort to futile attempts at logic or empty threats.

Research suggests that nearly half of our actions are habitual. So not only can you hack the habit loop to get better rest, but you can use this technique to change other troublesome behaviors. Once you've seen how to use the power of habit to your advantage, you can extrapolate it anywhere automatic behavior is in control. I know that while I was researching this topic, I learned to be a better parent. I hope you feel the same after reading this book.

How This Book Is Structured

This book is divided into three parts, reflecting the three steps you need to follow to help your child achieve independent sleep.

1. **The Fundamentals of Sleep and the Habit Loop.** In this part, I'm going to walk you through how sleep works in childhood and explain in detail the psychology of habit, which is the basis for improving your child's sleep. We'll then lay the groundwork for better sleep by addressing issues such as managing night feeding, transitioning your child to his own room or sleeping space, and soothing nighttime fears.

2. **The Bedtime Cue.** In the second part, we are going to rebuild your child's bedtime, which is the ultimate cue for a successful night of sleep and is the first step in successfully hacking the habit loop. You may feel inclined to skip this step, thinking that your bedtime ritual is just fine, but please don't. One hundred percent of the families we see in our Sleep Center benefit from some fine-tuning of their bedtime routine. We'll cover timing, sleep spaces, and flow. This is the beginning of the habit loop. If you are still tempted to skip this part, look at the science. When researchers in Yorkshire, England, studied the effects of consistent bedtimes, the benefits were startling. Children with consistent bedtimes in early childhood (at ages three and five) were more likely to perform better in terms of reading, math, and spatial skills. Moreover, these

effects appeared to be cumulative—the longer the irregular bedtime went on, the worse the effect.

3. **The Truth About Consequences.** This is the second step in hacking your child's sleep habits and will get you where you need to go—a good night's sleep for everyone. This part will cover the ways you respond to your child's behavior, and how you can change to help her sleep better. Some of these techniques will sound familiar—such as cry-it-out or extinction-based sleep training—and others will not. In some circles, the term "sleep training" has a bad reputation, but all the techniques in this book have solid evidence for both their safety and their effectiveness. Broadly, these methods are different ways to sleep train, and if you have tried and failed to sleep train, you will find a method here that is a better fit for your family. But make sure you've worked through Part Two first! Establishing bedtime as a clear and consistent cue will make these interventions much easier—even if you have failed before.

> Some great sleepers are born. Others are made.
> Let's make your child a great sleeper.

ACTION ITEMS

1. Start a sleep diary to track your child's sleep. I prefer sleep diaries based on a grid, as they give you a good high-level overview of what is going on. You can download some simple sleep diaries from my website at drcraigcanapari.com/nevertoolate.

2. Talk with your pediatrician about the possible medical causes of sleep problems, described in Chapter 2—this is low-hanging fruit. Sometimes a simple medical fix can either solve your child's sleep problems or make the behavioral changes recommended in this book go more smoothly. At the very least, you will not have the lingering doubt that you might be missing something.

3. Write down your intentions for improving your child's sleep. I know this sounds a bit hippy-dippy, but trust me, it works. Write down three benefits to yourself, and three for your child, of better sleep. Post this on your refrigerator and look at it every day, especially if you feel like things aren't going well or you want to give up.

PART ONE

THE FUNDAMENTALS OF SLEEP AND THE HABIT LOOP

TO UNDERSTAND HOW to fix your child's sleep, it's critical to understand why your family is struggling in the first place. In this section, we'll review the evolution of sleep in infancy (when many sleep problems begin) as well as discuss my Ten Commandments for Sleep Success for babies and parents.

Next, we'll move on to understanding how the psychology of habit is powering your child's current sleep problems, and how you are likely reinforcing this situation despite your best intentions otherwise.

Finally, we'll deal with three major habits that need to be addressed immediately—co-sleeping, nighttime feedings, and tantrums. Doing so will greatly improve the life of your family and lay the foundation for sleep success (or perhaps resolve your child's sleep problems entirely).

CHAPTER 1

THE BIOLOGY OF BEDTIME

How Children Sleep (and How to Make It Better)

GOALS

....

- Review the normal development of sleep in infancy.

- Understand how you can help your baby develop good sleep habits from birth.

- Learn about using a baby monitor, the timing of sleep training, and more.

ALTHOUGH THIS BOOK is focused on helping the parents of children one year old and up, understanding the evolution of sleep in infancy is critical to understanding how your child's sleep problems evolved, whether you have an infant, a toddler, or a school-age child. Many of the children I see in the Pediatric Sleep Center have "never been good sleepers," according to their parents. This chapter will help you understand why your toddler has been struggling with sleep since he came home from the hospital, and it will also help you set your newborn up for good sleep. Don't worry if you want to sleep train your baby. I'll show you how to do that too.

Sleep in the First Six Months of Life, and Beyond

When my older son was about six months of age, he had been sleeping through the night for a month or so. My wife and I were relieved to have so easily moved out of the sleep-deprived newborn months, during which he had slept in short bursts, waking at two- or three-hour intervals for feeding and diaper changes. At least half of infants naturally grow out of this pattern by five to six months and achieve what scientists have defined as "sleeping through the night"—sleep without interruption from 10:00 p.m. to 6:00 a.m. Then our son started to wake up first once and then two to three times a night to nurse. We were perplexed: What had happened to sleeping through the night?

Our routine had grown naturally out of the soothing techniques we'd used when he came home as a newborn: my wife would nurse our son to sleep, then place him in his crib. He could sleep through the night because he had reached an age where he did not need middle-of-the-night calories anymore and he was old enough to self-soothe. But we had become so comfortable in our little routine of nursing and rocking him to sleep that we missed the opportunity to put him to bed drowsy but awake. We'd created a bad sleep habit (technically called an "inappropriate sleep onset association"), which often causes these nocturnal awakenings. In Chapter 2, we'll talk about how this problem obeys the logic of habits, and in Chapter 7, I'll tell you what we did (in the section called "My Sleep-Training Mistakes").

Although my day job is dealing with the biology of sleep (and sleep problems) in children, I was still surprised to discover how quickly developmental changes in sleep can trip parents up. Understanding how your child's sleep changes as he grows will help you recognize why your child's sleep pattern changes so quickly in the first year. It will also help you understand the reasons behind the process in this book, and help you anticipate problems with your next child.

I'm not the first doctor to find my own experience in parenting useful. One of the fathers of sleep medicine, Nathaniel Kleitman, wrote a seminal paper on the development of sleep in infancy. In it, he included an illustration that, at first glance, looks like a series of lines and dots, almost like Morse code (see page 18). It was a different sort of code, however, one that tired parents have been trying to crack ever since: the sleep patterns for a child during the first six months of her life.

This particular child, Kleitman reports, "was a first child, and her parents were sufficiently indulgent to permit her to set her own sleep-wakefulness pattern." Rumor has it that the indulgent parent was Kleitman himself. (This illustration was clearly dear to him, as he used it to illustrate the cover of his book *Sleep and Wakefulness*, published ten years later.)

His study demonstrates some important truths about sleep in the first six months of life.

First, sleep is pretty chaotic in the first month or two. Do you clearly remember the first few weeks after you brought your child home from the hospital? I sure don't. Babies are physiologically hungry at night, leading to an apparent reversal of day and night. Fortunately, this resolves by about three weeks of age. After this, your child fairly quickly settles into a three- or four-hour cycle that typically follows a pattern of wake—feed—sleep. In the first few months, there is a wide range of normal sleep durations. Some babies may sleep twenty hours a day. Others may sleep ten to twelve hours per day, but these twelve hours usually don't occur together. Longer periods of wakefulness are distributed randomly— sometimes during the day and, unfortunately, sometimes at night.

Around three to four months of age, as they grow larger and

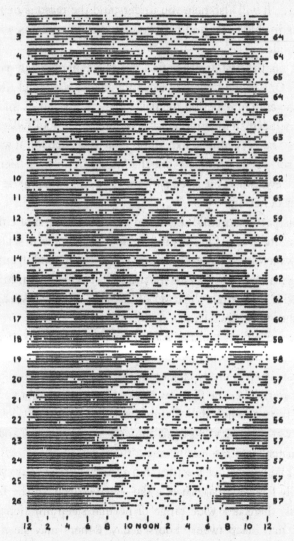

Each line of this study is a timeline from midnight to midnight in a given day (shown across the bottom). Solid lines represent sleep. White space represents wakefulness, and dots are feeds. The numbers going down the left side correspond to how many weeks have passed since birth. The numbers going down the right are the percentage of time spent sleeping in a twenty-four-hour period.

need less frequent feedings, babies can start having longer periods of sleep through the night. At this age, six to seven hours of continuous sleep is a pretty good stretch. It does not always occur during the nighttime hours, an effect of the dreaded day-night reversal. (Note to parents: This can be difficult to avoid. The best thing to do is make sure that your baby is exposed to natural light during the day and darkness at night, which will help her adjust to a natural rhythm.)

Around four months (weeks 16 and 17 on the graph), Kleitman's baby has a set pattern of persistent night sleeping and daytime waking. However, it's not until weeks 23 and 24 (around five months) when the child in the illustration has finally achieved the holy grail—pretty consistent nighttime sleep with minimal interruptions.

Kleitman's graph shows us a significant fact: after the first six months of life, most healthy children are able to sleep through the night. Many parents are racked with guilt about sleep training. But sleep research shows that children naturally move toward long periods of sleep at night. By following the plan in this book, you will be supporting your child's development by helping her to independent, uninterrupted sleep.

Six Months and Beyond: Settling into "Typical" Sleep

One of the most interesting things about sleep in infants from six months of age onward is how much their sleep resembles ours. When we study children in the Pediatric Sleep Center, we use electroencephalography (EEG) to study the different brainwave patterns that occur during the night. We use these patterns to classify the types (or stages) of sleep. The amount and timing of different stages of sleep in newborns differ significantly from what's seen in grown-ups like you and me, but by six months of age, the brain-wave patterns of babies look a lot like yours or mine, with a few subtle differences. Even children who struggle with sleep have the same brainwave patterns, and they sleep just like other children for most of the night (although their exhausted parents would say otherwise).

The stages of sleep are:

Stage 1: This is a brief stage, typically about 5 percent of the night, that occurs as you pass from wakefulness to sleep. It is very light, and during it a sleeper can be awoken easily. If you ever nod off and then jerk awake, you are in stage 1 sleep.

Stage 2: This is the most common stage, constituting about 50 percent of the night in children and adults. It is relatively light and dreamless.

Stage 3: This is also known as slow-wave or delta sleep, due to the large, slow waveforms noted on the EEG tracings. This is the deepest type of sleep, and the most refreshing. This is usually about 25 percent of the night in children and young adults, and is reduced in the elderly—this is why old people often endure insomnia. It is very difficult to wake a child in stage 3. If you have ever picked your child up from his car seat, changed his diaper, put him in his pajamas, and laid him down in his crib without waking him up, he was in stage 3. Since this stage tends to occur in the first half of the night, it explains why many children with sleep problems eventually go to sleep but then wake up and need Mom or Dad two to three hours later, just as their parents are climbing into bed. Stage 3 is also when sleep-walking and night terrors occur.

Rapid eye movement (REM) sleep: This stage accounts for about 20 percent of the night, and it is when vivid dreams occur. If you wake up out of REM sleep (for instance, if you hear your alarm in your dream and then you awaken), you'll feel wide awake, with none of the grogginess that occurs if, say, your screaming child wakes you up during stage 3. It is also when nightmares occur. During REM sleep, all of your skeletal muscles are paralyzed except for your diaphragm (the main breathing muscle) and your eye muscles. In the first few months of life, babies enter sleep through REM sleep. The paralysis during REM sleep in young infants is incomplete. That is why young babies frequently twitch, grunt, sigh, and briefly cry out right after they fall asleep. It is the characteristic back-and-forth eye movements that give REM sleep its name.

In the sleep laboratory, we use a road map of the night, called a *hypnogram*, to show the pattern of sleep during the night. Here's what a night of sleep should look like. Read the timeline from bedtime (left) to wake time (right).

WHAT A NORMAL NIGHT OF SLEEP SHOULD LOOK LIKE:

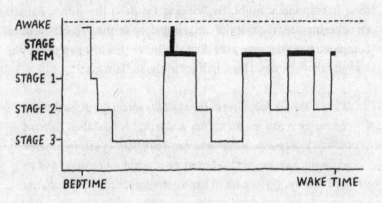

Note a few things: First, that deep period of slow-wave sleep in the beginning of the night. That's when you can transfer your child from car seat to crib without incident. The second is the vertical bar over the first REM period. During REM sleep, awakenings are both natural and common. We all experience them at night, but if your sleep environment is the way you arranged it to fall asleep at night, you usually go right back to sleep. (If you fell asleep in your bed and woke up on the floor of the bathroom, you would likely not just go back to sleep.) If you are only awake for five minutes, you won't remember this the next day.

Everyone has these brief awakenings, but a subset of infants will cry out during them. Sleep researchers call these babies "signalers," given that they seek attention when they wake up at night. Other babies are "self-soothers," meaning that they go back to sleep without calling out to Mom or Dad. You have some control over this. When researchers reviewed video of how parents put their children to bed, they found that children put to bed drowsy but awake at three months of age were more likely to self-soothe at night. Other factors that predicted better sleep in infants were more time spent sleeping in the crib (instead of the stroller, car seat, swing, or parental bed) in the first year of life, and parents who took a longer time to respond at night. In *Bringing Up Bébé*, the author Pamela Druckerman marvels at the amazing sleep of the French children compared with her own kids. She attributes this to a parenting philosophy that she describes, half-jokingly, as "la pause":

> When a French baby cries in the night the parents go in, pause, and observe for a few minutes. They know that babies' sleep patterns include movements, noises and two-hour sleep cycles, in between which the baby might cry. Left alone it might "self-soothe" and go back to sleep. If you dash in like an Anglophone and immediately

pick your baby up, you are training it to wake up properly. But if a French baby does wake up and cry properly on its own, it will be picked up. Result? French babies often sleep through the night from two months. Six months is considered very late indeed.

Parents need to allow their child a moment to go back to sleep before rushing into the room to offer a pacifier (or bottle, or breast) and thus reinforcing these awakenings. Such quick responses to fussing infants often form the basis of bad sleep habits, as we will discuss in Chapter 2.

A Timeline of Sleep, from Birth to Adolescence

If your child goes to sleep, sleeps through the night, and wakes up refreshed in the morning, she's likely getting enough sleep. If in doubt, check your child's typical sleep duration against the suggested numbers below.

Age	Sleep Needs (Total)	Nap Pattern	Notes
Newborn (0–3 months)	14–17 hours but can be more or less	Every 1–2 hours	60% of sleep occurs during the night and 40% during the day
Infant (4–11 months)	12–16 hours	3–4 hours per day	Naps decrease from 4–5 per day to 1–2 per day; many infants take very short naps multiple times per day, even at 9–10 months
Toddler (1–2 years)	11–14 hours	2–3 hours per day	Naps decrease from 2 to 1 per day around 18 months of age

Age	Sleep Needs (Total)	Nap Pattern	Notes
Preschooler (3–5 years)	10–13 hours	Usually eliminated during this age period	About 15% of 5-year-olds still nap
School age (6–12 years)	9–12 hours	None; if your child needs naps, he either is not getting enough sleep at night or could have a sleep disorder	
Teenagers (13–18 years)	8–10 hours	None	

Ten Commandments of Sleep Success in the First Year

Everyone's child is different. Some children sleep great no matter what. Some will struggle even if parents do everything perfectly. However, there are some best practices that will spare you a lot of wrecked nights if you follow them from the beginning. Trust me, I broke a few of them myself and lived to regret it.

1. The Best Time to Start a Bedtime Routine Is When You Bring Your Child Home from the Hospital

The second-best time is today. Children thrive on routine. (So do parents.) Newborns benefit as well, although the advantages are more for you in the first few weeks. Things feel chaotic when you bring your child home from the hospital, and a predictable bedtime routine helps anchor your day. For more on creating the best possible bedtime routine, go to Part Two. But right now, I would suggest keeping it simple, as I'll explain shortly.

2. If You Breast-feed, Teach Your Child to Take a Bottle Once Nursing Is Established

Like most pediatricians, I'm a huge fan of breast-feeding. There are too many benefits for mother and child to list here. However, I've seen many families fall into the trap of Mom nursing exclusively for the first few months, with the result that the child refuses anything but the breast. This makes it difficult for the whole family, as other adults are sidelined and Mom is stuck putting the baby down every night and dealing with every nighttime feeding. It can also greatly complicate Mom's return to work outside the home, if that is her plan. Once your milk supply is established, introduce a bottle, ideally given by your child's other parent, or by another adult caregiver. The best time for this is likely around four to six weeks of age, when your milk supply is fully established. Likewise, don't be shy about using a pacifier, even on day one. Despite claims to the contrary, they do not cause "nipple confusion" and keep babies from nursing. But they do help babies self-soothe and may reduce the risk of sudden infant death syndrome.

3. Make Sure That Bedtime Is Simple Enough That One Grown-up Can Do It

When my first son came home from the hospital, my wife and I did bedtime every night together—which was lovely, but it was pretty elaborate in terms of the bath, lotion application, song, story, rocking, and nursing. My second son did not have such an elaborate process, because we had son #1 to deal with as well, and it still worked fine. Babies don't need complex bedtimes. If bathtime feels overwhelming, do it at another time. Keep it simple: story, song, rocking, and put your baby down.

4. Make Sure That All the Adults in the Household Participate in Bedtime

I've heard the same story from tired parents (often the nursing mother), over and over: "My husband [or wife] can't put him down at night! Only I can do it." Like when only the mother can feed the baby (discussed earlier), this is a recipe for maternal burnout. Every parent or other caregiver should feel comfortable doing the bedtime routine and putting the child down at an early age. If you as the primary caregiver already feel stuck in this situation, you need to go out with friends for the evening. I promise you that Dad will figure it out. And don't be afraid to get a babysitter. Obviously, you will be nervous. If you can, start with a grandparent the first few times you go out.

5. Put Your Child to Bed Drowsy but Awake, Starting Around Three to Four Months

Try it out, both at bedtime and for naps. If it is a disaster the first time, pick your child up and try again in a week or two. Don't be afraid to let your child fuss a bit; this is natural. Hysterical screaming is another story at this age, however—this means that your child probably still needs you to help her fall asleep. You can try again in a week or so.

6. Don't Sprint into Your Child's Room at Night at the First Sound of Wakefulness

I remember hustling into my son's room at the slightest sound so that I could stuff the binky in his mouth and perhaps get back to sleep quickly. This led to him waking up more and more for the contact with me. Channel the French parent and remember that the random cry, burp, fart, or snort does not demand immediate attention. After the first few months, it's a great idea to let your child fuss a bit before you go in. Often these brief awakenings will self-resolve.

7. Don't Obsess over the Monitor

I can't believe the amount of technology being hawked to anxious parents these days. Babies' bedrooms are monitored to a degree that would astound a Cold War spymaster—temperature, movement, sound, ambient light levels, heart rate, and so on. I think that the majority of this technology is cumbersome, expensive, and unnecessary. Human infants have thrived for thousands of years without video monitors. Sure, you should be able to hear your child if she is distressed, but you don't need multi-sensor surveillance for this. Save the money and get an audio monitor. Parents often ask me questions like "I check on her with the monitor and sometimes she is wide awake and quiet during the night. What should I do?" My answer: "Turn off the monitor." For more on monitors, see page 34.

8. Talk with Your Pediatrician About the Need for Room Sharing in the First Year

I have grave concerns about the American Academy of Pediatrics (AAP) recommendation that parents room-share with infants for the first year of life to prevent SIDS. I think the evidence is weak and the potential for bad sleep habits is much higher. The majority of pediatricians I know agree, although they do share and discuss the recommendation with the families in their care. For further discussion on this and safe sleep in general, please talk to your pediatrician and also refer to the "Safe Sleep in Infancy" section of this chapter (page 29).

9. Sleep in Motion in the First Six Months Is OK, but After That, Be at Home

We loved our son's swing when he was a newborn because it would help him settle. A friend of mine used to drive to Starbucks to get her son to nap, and would drive around for hours to get him to stay asleep. In the first six months, I think this is fine for nap time. Any longer, however, and your child will start to develop a habit that will be hard to break. Of course, anyplace you have your child sleeping needs to be safe.

10. Naps Are Hard—but a Few Techniques Can Help

There's not as much research about addressing nap issues as there is about improving nighttime sleep. If you fix nighttime sleep, however, the naps tend to get better. In addition, as you go through the program for nighttime sleep in this book, you should follow a few principles when dealing with naps. (And for more on naps, see Chapters 5 and 9.)

- **Keep the nap prep short and sweet.** Your nap time ritual should be a scaled-down version of your bedtime routine. So if bedtime takes thirty minutes, fifteen to twenty minutes is as long as the nap time ritual should be.
- **Play with the timing.** After six months of age, try two to three hours after waking for nap #1, around midday for nap #2, and possibly a short nap around 3:00–4:00 p.m. If your child does not fall asleep after thirty minutes, get her up and wait until the next nap period to try again.
- **Avoid too much napping in the late afternoon.** For older children, don't let your child nap past 4:00 p.m. unless he can still fall asleep at his regular bedtime and sleep through the night.

- **Respect the nap.** Before I had children, I always wondered why my friends were so strict about the timing and duration of their children's naps. But then I had kids—and the cost of skipping naps became clear. My son would be miserable, and so would the rest of us. It won't surprise you that we quickly learned to maintain our nap times and bedtimes with an almost religious zeal.
- **Naps in motion (strollers, car seats, and swings), especially short ones, aren't as good as naps in a crib or bassinet.** The sleep quality is just not as deep, and this can cause a sleep onset association (see chapter 2).

For more on when naps should occur, see Chapter 5.

Safe Sleep in Infancy

No one likes to talk about sudden infant death syndrome (SIDS). It is a terrifying topic. I remember the first night home with my first son. I woke up the next morning when it was light out and was convinced that he had died in his sleep. Thankfully, he was fine— just a sound sleeper. But every parent of an infant has experienced this fear firsthand, and, sad to say, some parents have lost children to SIDS or accidental suffocation. These deaths occur in the first year of life, with the highest risk during the period from two to six months of age. Fortunately, these deaths are becoming less and less common, in great part because of the Back to Sleep campaign in the early 1990s, which urged parents to place infants to sleep on their back. This greatly reduces the risk of SIDS.

The American Academy of Pediatrics has recommended the following practices, which have been demonstrated to make sleep safer for babies:

- Put your child to sleep on her back only (once your child can roll over, this is moot).
- Use a firm mattress with no loose pillows, blankets, stuffed animals, or any other soft materials that can cause suffocation. I know those crib bumpers look cute, but they are unsafe. I would also avoid infant sleep positioners, as there is no evidence of safety or benefit.
- Avoid tobacco smoke, alcohol, or drug exposure during pregnancy and in infancy.
- Encourage use of a pacifier (if your child will take it) through at least six months of age.
- Obtain all regular childhood immunizations.
- Avoid overheating. Your child only needs one more layer than you are wearing.
- Share a room with your infant, but avoid bed sharing.

Of course, many families choose to co-sleep with their babies, and in many cultures parents share a bed with their infants and children as a matter of course. This is a complicated topic, to say the least. We pediatricians have stigmatized co-sleeping, to the point that many families do it furtively, without telling their physicians. But if you do wish to share a sleeping surface, it is critical that you do so safely.

It is clear that infants at high risk for SIDS *should not* share a bed with their parents. So if any of these conditions apply to you, you definitely should not share a bed:

- Your baby was born prematurely.
- You or your partner routinely uses alcohol or drugs prior to bed.
- Your baby's mother smoked during pregnancy, or any of the grown-ups in your house smoke.

Likewise, the choice of a sleeping surface is critical. Human infants did not evolve to sleep on a soft, pillow-top mattress surrounded by soft pillows and blankets. If you choose to co-sleep, do so on a firm mattress.

In 2016, when the AAP policy was updated, the room-sharing recommendation was strengthened. However, I think that this increases the risk of sleep onset association disorders. Further, the research the recommendation is based on predates the Back to Sleep campaign, so it's hard to know if the benefits are clear when the other recommendations are followed. A recent study showed that children who shared a room with their parents slept less than children who did not—and, more important, room-sharing parents were more likely to put their child in an unsafe sleeping situation (such as on a couch or chair). This suggests to me that room sharing may impose more risk than the AAP statement acknowledges.

If you are concerned about this recommendation, I advise you to discuss it with your pediatrician.

How Early Can You Sleep Train in Infancy?

Lately, a pediatric group in Manhattan made the news by recommending cry-it-out sleep training for two-month-old infants. While this may work, there is no research to support the approach. At two months of age, most infants aren't naturally sleeping through the night, whereas the behavior of many four- to six-month-olds suggests a natural shift.

The evidence is clear that sleep training doesn't hurt children (I'll review this evidence at length in Chapter 7), but the studies I'm aware of examined sleep-training techniques such as CIO at older ages; the best study of the long-term safety of CIO started with an intervention at seven months of age. I don't know if you can extrapolate these results back to an intervention at two months of age.

The first six months of life are a period of rapid neurological maturation. Nowhere is this more apparent than the change we see in sleep patterns. In the first several months of life, infants spend most of their time asleep, suggesting that sleep supports the critical developmental work of infancy. By three months, most babies have stable sleep patterns, with clear-cut, long nighttime sleep periods and relatively long periods of wakefulness. It seems to me that sleep interventions at four to six months help guide infants who are still struggling toward a biologically normal period of sustained sleep, whereas sleep training at two months of age takes babies who have normal patterns of wakefulness at night and forces them to behave like they are twice as old as they are. I agree that it is easier to sleep train a younger child, but I would recommend waiting until babies are four to six months of age.

Finding the Sweet Spot for Sleep Training in Infancy

So how do you find the sweet spot—the time to make this transition with minimal crying and fuss? There's no magic formula, and I firmly believe that every child's sleep can be improved at any age if they are struggling. However, I think four months of age is a good place to start. Your child may give you some signs that he is ready if, say, he has started sleeping for a longer sleep period at night (four to six hours, as opposed to waking every three hours). Another cue is when your child has been sleeping better, but then starts to wake up more frequently again—exactly what happened with my son. If you catch him at the right time, you can quickly sleep train with a minimum of fuss using the following method.

Unfortunately, with my son, we missed the signs. We were in a bit of denial when it was time to sleep train. For a few weeks, we kept waiting for it to get better—perhaps you have been there as well. But finally, my wife and I agreed that it was time for us to put him down drowsy but awake.

It wasn't pretty, but it worked. (See "My Sleep-Training Mistakes" in Chapter 7 for more details.) If I had to do it again, I would do it differently. When you have an infant, your options are limited. You can't use a sticker chart or talk your child into changing his behavior. But you can employ a strategy that I now recommend to parents of infants, which is an abbreviated version of what we do in the rest of the book.

- Follow the Ten Commandments on page 24.
- Pick a convenient date to start addressing this issue. Make sure that you leave yourself enough time to succeed, or give yourself enough "runway," as described in Chapter 2.
- Try a later bedtime (twenty to thirty minutes later). This will make your baby more tired, which is helpful.
- Try switching your bedtime routine to separate nursing/ feeding from sleep onset. Thus, instead of bath ▶ story ▶ song ▶ nursing ▶ crib, change the order to nursing ▶ bath ▶ story ▶ song ▶ crib. This is a great opportunity for the dad (or non-nursing partner) to take a more active role in bedtime. In Chapter 6, I'll tell you how to use the Bedtime Funnel to refine your child's bedtime, but for infants, moving feeding earlier in the bedtime sequence is critical.
- Place the baby in the crib drowsy but awake.
- If your baby fusses a bit, try leaving the room and see how it goes. If it is a disaster, you can stop and try again in a few weeks, or you can choose to try "cry it out" or "camping out." Details of these methods are in Chapter 8.

Once this bedtime routine is established, the nighttime awakenings will extinguish on their own. Frequent feeding at night will reinforce them. For more on dealing with feedings, check out Chapter 3.

Your child should start to fall asleep more easily in three to five days if you are consistent. Don't be surprised if things get a little bit worse before they get better—this phenomenon is called the "extinction burst" and is covered more in Chapter 3.

IN THE CASE OF BABY MONITORS, LESS IS BEST

Here's a question a mom asked on my website:

My thirteen-month-old wakes up several times a night, a fact I know because of the baby monitor next to my bed but wouldn't know otherwise. (I'm working on weaning myself from the monitor!) For these wake-ups, he puts himself back to sleep with minimal issue, never requiring me to go into his room. What should I do about this?

My answer: turn off the monitor once you get into bed, provided that you can hear your child if she is in distress. Most parents sleep in a room near their child, well within earshot. You don't need to wake up if your child is softly cooing in the crib. This happens more commonly than you may think, and rushing in the second you hear your child move is certain to reinforce a night-waking habit.

There is another sort of infant monitor that tracks information like heart rate, sound, and motion. These devices prey on the worst fears of parents, and they have not been shown to reduce the likelihood of SIDS. (Even medical-grade monitors prescribed by doctors don't make sleep safer.) What they do instead is either give parents a false sense of security or make them nervous wrecks by producing endless false alarms. I did not buy such a device and would not recommend that you do.

Sleep is challenging in year one. You have a limited amount of control, especially in the beginning, and a lot of the sleep disruption is natural and to be expected. By following the steps above, you will lay the groundwork for successful sleep for everyone at home. However, despite our best efforts, disruptive sleep patterns can take root. (Or perhaps you are already in the midst of them.) In Chapter 2, we'll talk about how bad sleep habits develop. Understanding the nature of these habits will allow you to change them.

ACTION ITEMS

1. If you have an infant, look for cues that he is ready to sleep independently. Is he naturally sleeping for longer periods? Or did his sleep improve, and then revert to several awakenings at night? Keep a simple sleep diary so you don't miss these signs.

2. Make sure that you are following the Ten Commandments of Sleep Success (see page 24).

3. Ensure that your child sleeps in a safe, secure place: without soft blankets or pillows and on a firm mattress.

4. If you use a baby monitor, consider whether you can do without. Can you hear your child if she is in distress at night, without the aid of a monitor?

5. If your child is four months or older, try putting him to bed drowsy but awake.

CHAPTER 2

HACKING THE HABIT LOOP

The Key to Solving Bad Sleep

GOALS

- Understand how common sleep problems obey the logic of habits.

- Recognize how your child's sleep problems trigger habits of your own that continue the cycle of bad sleep.

- Avoid pitfalls that make it challenging to create better sleep habits.

AS A PARENT, you need to remember two things. First, every child can be a good sleeper. Second, most kids with sleep difficulties have just one major obstacle to overcome: their parents. In this chapter, we'll discuss the ways in which bad sleep is a bad habit, describe some of the most common bad habits, and explain why changing *your* habits is central to changing your child's.

Parents: The Major Obstacle to Success

In Chapter 1, we talked about the fact that it's perfectly natural for children to wake up at night during infancy. For some lucky parents, their children sleep well no matter what they do. Other parents work hard to sleep train their baby and are successful. But sometimes sleep issues aren't easily addressed in infancy—or perhaps they resolve, then start up again.

By the time a child reaches six months of age without sleeping through the night, his parents are depleted and just trying to survive. And exhausted parents often reinforce the behaviors they don't like by repeatedly indulging them, taking the path of least resistance to get their child to sleep. You may not like your child waking up every night at 2:00 a.m.—but bringing him into your bed ensures that he will continue to do so.

Here's a hard truth about parenting: *you can't control your child's behavior directly.* Parents of teenagers know this very well, but if your child is small, you may have the illusion of control. If your two-year-old is reluctant to get in the car, you can pick her up and place her where you want her to go. However, you aren't really changing behavior when you force your child to do something against her will. Likewise, you haven't changed anything if you give in and do it for her. For example, here's a conversation I had with my son last week (and many times previously):

Me: OK, buddy. We're going out. Can you put on your shoes?

Son: I don't want to go out.

Me: But we're going out for ice cream!

Son: I can't find my shoes.

Me: They are right there in front of you.

Son: *(Makes halfhearted attempt to put shoes on.)* I don't like these socks!

Me: *(Goes and gets new socks, put socks and shoes on, reflects on failure as a parent.)*

We all have banged our head against the wall of our child's stubbornness—and getting a child to sleep independently often feels particularly impossible. Why do so many devoted and otherwise competent parents have such a hard time? Every parent who comes into the Sleep Center has tried and failed at sleep training. But there is hope, because it is much easier to change our own behavior than someone else's. We just need to change the way we look at sleep problems in children.

Bad Sleep Is a Bad Habit

Many parents' difficulties in managing their children's sleep problems stem from one frequently overlooked fact: bad sleep is a bad habit. The parents who come to my clinic find this simple truth surprisingly helpful. It's not that sleep experts don't refer to habits—Dr. Weissbluth's very successful book is called *Healthy Sleep Habits, Happy Child*, after all. But most sleep experts have very little to say about the psychology of habit and how it helps and hinders us. Why do we repeat the same behavior, even when we know it is not in our best interest? And how can we stop? How do we replace bad habits with good ones? We are all familiar with habits, but the mechanisms that power them aren't as well known. When you understand how habits function, as behavioral scientists do, they become much easier to change. So, how can foggy-brained, busy parents harness habit to improve their children's sleep?

Habits are behaviors that occur automatically, without conscious effort, over and over again. You form a habit by performing the same action repeatedly in response to a certain trigger. Habits can be positive (starting your day with a run) and help us by removing decisions and reducing response times in certain situations (like pressing the brakes in your car when the car in front of you slows down). However, habits can also cause the automatic repetition of undesirable behaviors, such as going out for a cigarette after lunch, or eating a bag of chips every time you sit down to watch television.

Researchers who work on the psychology of habit explain that every habit has three main parts: (1) a trigger, or *cue*, which prompts (2) the routine *behavior* that we identify as the habit, and (3) a reinforcing *consequence*, which rewards the habit and makes it likely to occur again. This three-part "habit loop" (cue, behavior, and reinforcing consequence) keeps on playing, for better or worse—unless we make a special effort to stop it.

Here's an example. If your child cries for you at night, these events are triggered by normal biologic awakenings (cue). This results in the behavior of her crying out for you and the consequence of you going into her room and rocking her back to sleep.

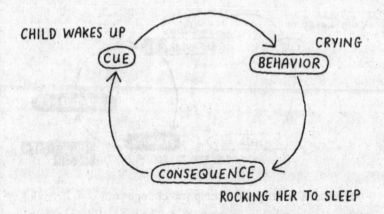

Repeating the habit loop imprints distinct patterns within your brain—literally hardwiring you to continue the behavior. This is why habits are so difficult to change. And stress increases the likelihood of habit formation. That's why tired parents often fall into the same patterns over and over—your tired brain forms habits to reduce your need to think.

We tend to think of habits in individuals, but they can also occur in groups, including families. If your family sits down to eat dinner together every night, that is a habit. Likewise, if you argue with your child about eating her vegetables at every one of those dinners, that's a habit, too. Such patterns actually represent the interlocking habits of different family members. Habits like sleep problems do not occur in a vacuum. Let's take the example of your child waking up at night. Your child has a normal nighttime awakening (cue) and cries (behavior), leading to your going in and rocking her to sleep (consequence). This is actually reinforcing a second habit loop—your own. When you hear your child cry out (cue), you rush in and rock her to sleep (behavior) so you can go back to sleep (consequence).

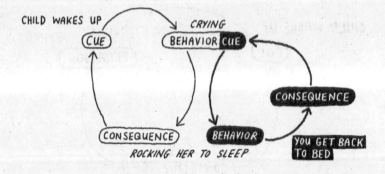

This book is designed to help you change your own behavior to create new sleep habits in your child. The key will be recognizing that *your* behavior is the consequence of your child's action and thus likely reinforces the sleep-related behaviors you want to fix. For the purposes of simplicity, other chapters will largely focus on your child's habit loop, specifically the cues and consequences of her behaviors. But to do that, first you need to look at your own habit loop and how it influences your child.

Changing the Loop

In his 2012 book *The Power of Habit*, Charles Duhigg explored how habits are created and how we can break them. He describes what he calls the Golden Rule of habit-breaking: don't mess with the cue or consequence, but change the routine in the middle. Duhigg experimented on himself. He'd discovered that his craving for a chocolate cookie occurred each day around 3:30 (the cue), at which point he would go to the cafeteria and spend ten to fifteen minutes chatting with colleagues while eating the cookie before returning to his desk. The cookie was the habit he wanted to break, because he was gaining weight. But he realized that the consequence he craved was socializing rather than sugar. So he replaced the midafternoon cookie with a routine schmooze session minus the cookie, and before long he had successfully reset the habit loop.

But habit-breaking and habit-making are different in the case of young children, for two critical reasons. First, you will likely have to initiate any changes. Your son won't raise his hand and say, "You know, Dad, I've given it some thought and I'm going to stop coming into your room at 4:00 a.m. every morning." (I'm the parent of an early riser, so you can trust me on this.) The second reason is more subtle. Duhigg's Golden Rule works well for adults who can make the conscious decision to change their routine. But if you want to change your child's habit, you can't just replace it with another one. You need to work indirectly—by changing your own routine behavior (and thus your child's consequence). This is because (repeat after me) *you can't change your child's behavior directly*. If she wants to cry, shout, or throw things, you can't stop this. If you don't like something she does over and over (that is, a bad habit), you can intervene upstream with cues or downstream with consequences.

Take a simple example from the world of sleep. Your child wakes up when he sees sunlight outside his window (the cue), then gets out of bed and comes into your room (the routine behavior). You pull him into bed with you (that's *his* reinforcing consequence but *your* routine behavior). You can ask or tell your child not to get out of bed at 5:00 a.m. (and probably have done so), but I bet that hasn't worked. You will increase your chances of success significantly, however, if you control the cue (by, for example, putting blackout shades up in his room) and the consequence (by bringing him back to his room every time he gets up). Note that you are changing his behavior by revising your own. Sometimes it will be enough to change the cue; other times you'll need to tackle both. Dr. Alan Kazdin, a Yale psychologist, has shown that by using both cue and consequence tools you can shape behavior even in children with severe behavioral problems. We'll talk more about Dr. Kazdin's methods in Chapter 8.

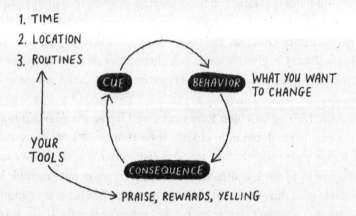

The truth is that we parents often inadvertently reward the very behaviors we want to change. Here's something even more frustrating: punishment can reinforce undesirable behaviors. Do you remember that time your child did something annoying, you yelled at your child to stop it, and he instantly stopped doing it, forever? Me neither. Focusing attention on that annoying behavior often makes it more likely to continue. Why? Because parental attention—no matter whether it's positive or negative—is often the best possible reward.

In other words, changing your child's habit means changing your own. Don't be discouraged by this. Parents power their child's sleep habit loop—which means they have the power to reset it, too.

Two Habit Loops: Frequent Waking and Bedtime Resistance

Before we can change habit loops, we have to be able to recognize them. Here I'll describe the two most common behavioral sleep problems. I would wager your child has at least one of them. Note that I am simplifying these loops here to show just your child's habit loop and not your own, for the purposes of clarity. (The work of changing these habits will happen in Part Two, when we work on the bedtime cue, and Part Three, where we talk about changing consequences.)

Sleep Onset Association Disorder, or "Why Does My Kid Wake Up Screaming Every Night?"

It's been a long evening in the Smith household. Ayesha is fourteen months old. Every night since she was an infant, her parents have rocked her to sleep and then put her in her crib at around 8:00 p.m. Her parents sit down to watch some television and try to relax, but they are dreading the night ahead. Just when they get into bed, around 11:00 p.m., they hear Ayesha crying out. They rush into her room to rub her back so that she will fall asleep more quickly. These awakenings occur for the rest of the night, every sixty to ninety minutes. When she gets up for the day at 5:30 a.m., Ayesha is irritable and her parents are exhausted—and her parents don't have the luxury of taking two naps today. This might look like a night waking problem, but it originates at bedtime. She has what's technically called "behavioral insomnia of childhood, sleep onset association subtype."

Remember in Chapter 1, when I told you what a normal night of sleep looks like? In a child who falls asleep by himself, it looks like this:

WHAT A NORMAL NIGHT OF SLEEP SHOULD LOOK LIKE:

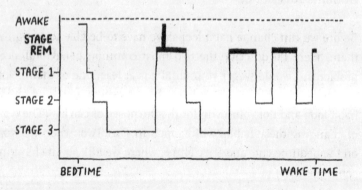

The vertical bar above the first REM period represents a natural awakening. We all have them, but we typically don't remember them as long as conditions when we wake are the same as when we fell asleep. If a child is used to falling asleep on his own, he won't signal to his parents when he wakes at night.

Children with inappropriate sleep onset associations need Mom or Dad present to fall asleep—just like Ayesha. Then, every time Ayesha wakes up, she finds that no parent is there, she cries out, and her parents come in to help her go back to sleep.

WHAT YOUR NIGHT OF SLEEP LOOKS LIKE:

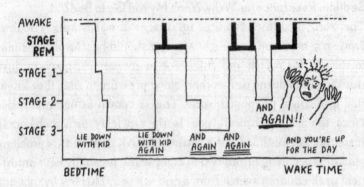

Sleep onset associations obey the habit logic. The cue is Ayesha waking up without Mom or Dad present. The behavior is crying out. And the consequence is attention from Mom or Dad. But Ayesha's parents have a habit of their own to break. Her crying cues them to rush in (behavior), and they are rewarded with a return to sleep for the whole family (consequence). Parents view the awakenings as the problem, but they are a symptom of the primary issue: their child has not learned to fall asleep by herself at bedtime.

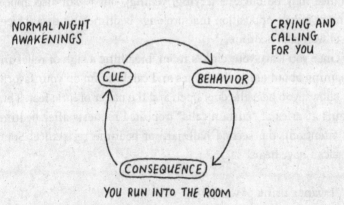

Bedtime Resistance, or "Why Won't My Kid Go to Bed?"

The word "bedtime" conjures up images of warm milk, cuddles, footie pajamas, and *Goodnight Moon*. It should be a lovely capstone to the day for parent and child. For many parents, however, just thinking of bedtime causes their blood pressure to rise; they know that it means a prolonged battle. This is known as bedtime resistance, though it technically goes by the unwieldy term "behavioral insomnia of childhood, limit setting type." Kids with this problem tend to range in age from two to eight years. It usually isn't prominent until children switch from a crib to a bed. This is why moving a child who has sleep problems from a crib to a bed is a bad idea—it can worsen preexisting sleep problems. (You'll learn more about the crib-to-bed transition in Chapter 4.)

The first hallmark of this disorder is prolonged fighting and struggling around bedtime. In some kids, this starts around the time of transitioning from post-dinner activities to bedtime activities. (In my house, this means going upstairs for a bath.) Other children wait to complain until they are in their rooms. The resistance may be obvious (crying, yelling), but it can also appear as more subtle opposition that prolongs bedtime and delays sleep onset well past bedtime.

Once you leave your child's room, breathing a sigh of relief and dreaming about doing the dishes and catching up on your favorite TV shows, you hear the door open and the patter of little feet. Thus begins a series of "curtain calls" (repeated requests after bedtime for attention), the second hallmark of bedtime resistance. Some classics I have heard:

"I want a drink of water."

"I need another hug."

"Will you rub my back some more?"

"Another story."

"I need to go to the bathroom."

"I'm scared" (without any apparent fear or distress).

"I need to go to the bathroom again."

"Can you check the closet and make sure there are no
    monsters in there?"

"I really need to go to the bathroom. I promise it's the last
    time."

(NPR's *Morning Edition* once described perhaps the best curtain call ever: a little boy with a prosthetic eye would regularly remove it and throw it on the floor, knowing that his parents would come running as soon as they heard it rolling around. Checkmate.)

Now, every parent has had a child try to delay bedtime a bit or encountered a rare curtain call. That is perfectly normal. Bedtime resistance, however, is characterized by prolonged delay of sleep onset, often more than an hour or two past the desired bedtime.

This fits neatly in our habit template: The cue is starting bedtime. The behavior is the arguing, curtain calls, and tantrums that ensue. And the consequence is the way you respond.

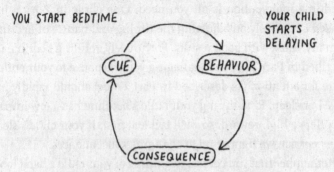

YOU START BEDTIME   YOUR CHILD
                                     STARTS
                                     DELAYING

CUE → BEHAVIOR → CONSEQUENCE

YOU ENGAGE BY REWARDING OR FIGHTING

If your child has this issue, I guarantee that the way you respond is reinforcing the bedtime battles. Maybe you give in. Maybe you argue. Maybe you lose your temper. Clearly, none of that is working.

WHAT IF MY CHILD FIGHTS BEDTIME AND THEN WAKES UP MULTIPLE TIMES AT NIGHT?

In the classic form, kids with bedtime resistance do not have problems with staying asleep. However, many of them may develop inappropriate sleep onset associations. A child may fight bedtime until his dad relents and rubs his back until he falls asleep, then he wakes up multiple times needing his dad to rub his back again. This combination of sleep onset disorder and bedtime resistance is the most common behavioral sleep type that I treat.

The Bedtime Solution

The secret to understanding both issues is that the problem in either case is bedtime. This is your maximum point of leverage for behavior change. And you have a lot more energy and willpower at bedtime than you will at midnight (or 2:00 a.m., or 4:00 a.m.). Often a bedtime intervention is all you need. One clinic in Zurich has focused exclusively on adjusting the timing and nature of bedtime for many years, with good results. Fortunately, refining bedtime (as described in Part Two) and managing your response to your child's desire for attention (as described in Part Three) should rapidly improve her sleep. Fine-tuning your child's bedtime has a low impact and offers a high reward, so we'll tackle it first. If your child's sleep issues persist, we'll move on to changing consequences.

Remember that you control two-thirds of your child's habit loop. You have the power to make changes—though, as with breaking any habit, you'll need to be consistent, patient, and determined.

When It's Not a Habit: Medical Issues and Sleep

One of the first things I do at the Sleep Center when assessing children with poor sleep is to look for medical conditions that may be causing or contributing to their difficulties. Why is this? First, often we find that treating a hidden or undertreated medical issue will fix sleep problems or make them a lot better. Second, some medical issues can doom even the best behavioral interventions to fail. Finally, parents need to have confidence that medical issues are not the cause of their child's sleep problem.

There are certain common disorders that can disrupt sleep:

- **Obstructive sleep apnea** is characterized by snoring, gasping, and choking at night. It is caused by recurrent obstruction of the upper airway (between the nose and the voice box). The most common cause in children is large tonsils and adenoids, although other medical causes (such as obesity) can be a factor. If your child snores most nights, discuss this with your pediatrician. She may elect to send you to an ear, nose, and throat physician, or order an overnight sleep test.

- **Restless leg syndrome** is also common in children, and it is frequently underdiagnosed. This syndrome occurs in one out of fifty kids. If your child seems fidgety or complains that her legs bother her at night, it may be worth discussing with your pediatrician. Common complaints include aches, "creepy-crawly" sensations, "too much energy," or feeling like the legs are hot. Often all that is needed is treatment with iron if your child's ferritin level (which your doctor can check with a blood test) is less than 40 ng/mL. Note that iron therapy should be managed by a doctor, as iron overdose can be dangerous. Sometimes other medications may be helpful as well. Some children with restless leg may also have rhythmic movements, called periodic limb movements of sleep, which may be detected on overnight sleep testing. These can also contribute to restless sleep and cause nighttime awakenings.

- **Parasomnias** are conditions in which your child acts like she is awake during sleep. These include sleep talking, sleepwalking, and night terrors. More on these later.

Other medical disorders can present with sleep issues during the night:

- **Cough at night** may be due to poorly controlled asthma, postnasal drip from allergies, or acid reflux.
- **Belly pain** can be associated with acid reflux, food allergies, milk sensitivity, or constipation.
- **Itchy skin** from eczema can result in marked sleep disruption.

If you suspect that your child might be experiencing any of these issues, please talk to your pediatrician. If necessary, you might be directed to overnight sleep testing, in which technicians monitor a night of your child's sleep to look for any underlying issues.

Things That Go Bump in the Night: Night Terrors, Sleepwalking, and Sleep Talking

The most common parasomnias have several characteristics in common:

- **They usually (but not always) occur in the first half of the night.** Most commonly they are seen a few hours after bedtime. This is because they emerge from the deepest kind of sleep, slow-wave or stage 3 sleep.

- During these events, children may be agitated and seem confused. They are usually difficult to console, and if you try to talk with them, the conversation is normally nonsensical.
- Children usually do not have difficulty going back to sleep after these events. (Although you may.)
- Generally, your child will not remember these events the next day.
- There is often a family history of similar events in first-degree relatives (parents and siblings).
- Usually (but not always) these events resolve by early adolescence.
- Events occurring in teenagers and adults tend to be longer and more severe.

Night terrors really freak parents out. All of a sudden, you hear your child screaming at the top of his lungs. You rush to his room to see what's wrong, and your child doesn't seem to see you. He may scream your name, but any effort to comfort him is in vain, and actually seems to agitate him further. Evidence of the fight-or-flight response (sweating, heart pounding, dilated pupils) is common. Eventually (usually in about ten minutes), the screams become sobs, and your child falls back to sleep. He doesn't remember it the next morning, but you sure do. These events are relatively uncommon, occurring in about 6 percent of children.

Sleepwalking, or somnambulism, is the act of walking around during slow-wave sleep. Children usually seem calm, to the point where a casual observer may think that the child is awake. One of the most common manifestations is your child wordlessly materializing at your bedside in the middle of the night, but not really seeming "all there." Less commonly, children may be agitated. It's important to remember that sleepwalkers can perform complex tasks such as unlocking doors or turning on the stove. Sleepwalkers can get injured if they get out of the house. Sleepwalking occurs in 15 percent of kids at some point; a much smaller proportion (1–6 percent) will have events at least once per week.

Confusional arousals are the less interesting, milder-mannered version of night terrors and sleepwalking. The timing is similar to the events above, and these events will usually present as some moaning, talking, and maybe a little light thrashing in bed. They typically last longer than night terrors—a five-to-fifteen-minute duration is common—but are milder.

Sleep talking (or somniloquy) is really common—so common, in fact, that I'm not convinced that it is a disorder per se. However, like all of these parasomnias, it can occur more commonly in children with disorders that result in sleep fragmentation, such as obstructive sleep apnea.

How do you treat these behaviors? Generally, if the behavior is infrequent, there's little cause for concern. However, frequent or severe episodes should be assessed by your physician. Consider the following steps:

- Make sure your child gets adequate sleep, as sleep deprivation is a clear trigger.
- Ensure a safe sleeping environment. At home, have double-locked doors (where you need a key to get out) or deadbolts out of children's reach. When traveling, consider bringing along a portable door alarm.
- Give your child sedating medication only in severe cases or when a night episode might be dangerous. (Obviously, this should be prescribed and supervised by your child's physician.)
- Try scheduled awakenings, a technique where parents wake children up nightly, usually about thirty minutes prior to the

typical time when the night terror or sleepwalking episodes occur. Doing this nightly for a month seems to reduce the frequency and severity of these events. You need to wake your child up to the point where he or she is able to have a conversation with you. There are two possible downsides. One is that on rare occasions scheduled awakenings may trigger an event. The other is that the awakenings can contribute to sleep deprivation.

Parental Pitfalls

OK, so now we understand what a habit is. It should be easy to create good sleep habits, right? Well, not exactly. First, you need to recognize how you accidentally created the bad habits that led to your child's poor sleep. These pitfalls can thwart your best-intentioned attempts to improve your child's behavior. I'll describe them briefly here but will address them in more detail in Chapter 7.

Inconsistency
Inconsistency around sleep is the most common driver of bad sleep habits, and the most common reason that sleep training fails. This is an issue with both cues and consequences. Here are some examples:

- Your child's bedtime occurs at different times throughout the week. Ditto for naps. It's OK to have a little bit of variability, but these events should generally happen at the same time every day.
- You and your partner do bedtime differently—say, Mom lies down with Beth until she falls asleep, but Dad leaves right after he turns out the light.

- You *sometimes*:
  - Bring your child into your bed when she wakes up at night.
  - Fall asleep next to your child at bedtime.
  - Go into your child's room twenty times at bedtime in response to a laundry list of demands ("One more story!" "One more hug!" "Close the closet!" "Take me to the bathroom to pee!").

TWO HOUSEHOLDS: A MAJOR CAUSE OF SLEEP INCONSISTENCY

If you are separated from your partner, your child likely sleeps in two households. If your child has varying routines and rules around sleeping, problems can ensue and worsen an already stressful situation. This can take many forms. Perhaps your child co-sleeps in one home but not the other, or has a different bedtime. These are thorny problems to address, especially as different parenting styles may have been a factor in the separation. I firmly believe that parents have the best interests of their child at heart, but they may differ in their beliefs about what is important or how to achieve it. If you are struggling with this, I encourage you to sit down with the other parent. Say, "I'm concerned about our daughter's sleep. I'm worried that you and I are sending different messages to her every night and this is making it hard for her to sleep well. I know you want her to sleep well. Can we talk about making nighttime the same at both of our homes so she doesn't get confused?" You both will likely have to compromise. Writing out the plan may be helpful. If this continues to be an issue, I encourage you to involve your child's pediatrician, a child psychologist, or a social worker.

As you go through this book, be conscious of each change in your child's routine, and follow your plan the same way, every night. This is especially true with how you start the night. Your child's bedtime needs to be a smart system that you activate at the same time each night. Which is not to say that your bedtime ritual should be mechanical or soulless, or devoid of cuddling or fun, but only that it should be clear and consistent, so that when your resolve weakens (understandably; you're a parent, you're super-tired!), you can rely on the program's automatic pilot to see you through. That is what a good habit does: it kicks in and carries you along just when you need it most.

Giving Up Too Soon

Sometimes your child's sleep will get worse before it gets better, especially when you are trying to get your child to sleep solo if she is used to falling asleep with a parent in the room. There is even a ridiculous name for this phenomenon: the "extinction burst" (because it occurs most commonly with cry-it-out sleep-training methods, technically called extinction sleep training). It means that what feels like the low point, when your child's sleep becomes more difficult than ever and the crying or fussing increases, is in fact the turning point, when improved sleep is right around the corner.

This is why you need to plan for success by leaving yourself enough runway. A plane needs a clear, long runway to take off. Likewise, for sleep training you need to have a stretch of time without major disruptions in your routine. If you have any of the following events planned in the next month, either rearrange your schedule or start sleep training after this:

- When your in-laws are visiting
- Right before a vacation (especially if you will be crossing time zones with your child)
- When your child is suffering from a cold, or teething, or working on another developmental task such as potty training or learning to walk

- Immediately before or after a new sibling is born
- Around the time of a big work deadline
- Right before you move to a new home

You should plan to stick with the bedtime interventions in this book for a few weeks. Changing your child's behavior (and your own) may take about a month, although you should see improvement generally within a week or two. For younger kids (less than a year), change may happen more quickly—sleep training my six-month-old took a week.

Lacking the Energy to Deal

Let's face it. You're tired. You have small kids with sleep problems. Parents, especially single mothers, are among the most sleep-deprived people in America—according to the Centers for Disease Control, 44 percent of single moms report that they average less than seven hours of sleep per night. Single dads and parents in two-parent families fare slightly better but are still struggling. Many of the families I see are horribly sleep deprived. Once I called a cab for a mom who was falling asleep in the Sleep Center.

If you are exhausted (and I suspect most readers of this book are), the last thing you want to do is argue with your child at bedtime or deal with crying in the middle of the night. I understand this. That's why I have structured this book to protect your sleep as much as possible. This process is designed so that you only need to make one change at a time. Moreover, most of the steps occur during the times you would be awake anyway—predominantly at bedtime. However, I guarantee that there will be low moments as you go through this process. If your resolve wavers, revisit your goals for creating better sleep for you and your child, and try to push through.

ACTION ITEMS

1. What are the sleep habits you want to break? Waking at night to feed? Early morning awakenings? Fighting at bedtime? Think about the cue that may be triggering these behaviors and whether the way you respond could accidentally be reinforcing your child's sleep problems. (You can download a double habit worksheet from drcraigcanapari .com/nevertoolate, which I encourage you to fill out.)

2. Think about the pitfalls listed in this chapter. Which have you fallen prey to in the past? How are you going to avoid them in the future?

3. Are you feeding your child during the night, or sharing a sleeping space with her? If so, go to Chapter 3. Otherwise, feel free to proceed to Chapter 4.

CHAPTER 3

SMOOTHING THE PATH

Habits to Address Before Sleep Training Begins

GOALS

....

- Address two common barriers to successful night sleep: bed sharing and night feeding.

- Learn how to manage tantrums, which can disrupt bedtime and night sleep.

BEFORE WE CAN improve your child's sleep habits, there are a few nighttime habits that some families need to address first. If you are co-sleeping, night feeding, or a combination of the two, changing these behaviors will build a foundation for better sleep. In this chapter, I'll show you how to do this as painlessly as possible. Tantrums are another destructive habit loop and can both intensify in the daytime during sleep training and be disruptive during bedtime or night awakenings. *If your child does not feed between bedtime and wake time and you are happy with where he sleeps, you can move on to Part Two, although you might find the section "Don't Let Tantrums Derail Your Plans" in this chapter useful.*

The Problem with Attachment Parenting

There is one constellation of sleep complaints that I see over and over—in comments on my website, in emails sent to me, and in the clinic. Here's a sample comment from my website:

> I have co-slept with my fifteen-month-old since birth. She wakes up multiple times during the night to nurse and will not go back to sleep until I feed her. My husband has given up sleeping in our bed because our child moves around so much. We've tried to sleep train in the past, but it was a disaster! Now I'm worried I've ruined my child's sleep. Can you help me?

How do so many of us end up in this predicament, and why do we find it so difficult to extricate ourselves?

The short answer is attachment parenting. The term originated in the 1960s work of the psychologist Mary Ainsworth, who demonstrated, against the conventional wisdom of the day, that responsive mothers provided children with the confidence to successfully explore the world. Dr. Ainsworth and her colleagues encouraged a parenting style that was warm and nurturing, and used the word "attachment" to describe the relationship between mother and child.

In the early 1990s, Dr. William Sears and his wife, Martha Sears, popularized the idea of "attachment parenting" with their bestseller *The Baby Book*. Dr. Sears, a pediatrician, espoused a style of parenting that included bed sharing with children throughout childhood, carrying your child everywhere (otherwise known as "baby wearing"), and on-demand nursing. The Searses offered an alternative to mainstream parenting practices that resonated with many guilty parents in two-career households who were trying to replicate the benefits of having a stay-at-home parent. Its influence has not diminished, and at this point, a whole generation of families has subscribed to the attachment parenting philosophy.

I agree with the Searses in many ways. You should pay attention to your child's needs and do what you feel is right. Here's my problem with the Sears philosophy: there is little room for the needs of the parents. Parents, especially mothers, are expected to soothe their children without limit. What happens if you decide that you need your child to sleep through the night because you are exhausted? Well, according to Dr. Sears, sleep training your child (specifically, any methods associated with crying) could result in brain damage. Specifically, he has posited that "excessive" crying floods the brains of babies with stress hormones (such as cortisol) and makes it so "nerves won't form connections to other nerves and will degenerate." This is the basis of the argument you may hear that sleep training harms babies. And that's how we end up with parents feeling trapped in a co-sleeping arrangement that doesn't afford anyone a good night's rest or in a cycle of frequent night feeding.

Honestly, this is ludicrous. Babies cry all the time. So do little kids. My six-year-old woke me up the other day, crying because he found an ant on his donut when he helped himself to breakfast. There was no evidence of brain damage afterward. In 2012, a reporter from *Time* magazine called the authors of the papers Dr. Sears referenced to support his conclusions about the ill effects of crying. The majority of them strongly disagreed with Dr. Sears's conclusions. For example, one of the studies examined children who displayed persistent crying during infancy, and the researchers associated such crying with developmental problems. However, the authors noted that the quality of maternal care provided to the child did not affect the crying; in short, the crying reflected an underlying problem, not a parenting style. Some of the other research examined children who experienced persistent abuse and neglect, not those who were crying in the context of routine activity. (For more on why sleep training is safe, please refer to Chapter 7.)

To be fair to Dr. Sears, he is not against all behavioral interventions to encourage better sleep. However, "sleep training" and "crying it out" have become virtually synonymous, so advocating against one becomes an indictment of the other, however unintentionally. Moreover, if you want to improve your child's sleep, it's unlikely that you will avoid his crying altogether. This book is structured to minimize your child's tears (and your own), but let's be clear: behavior change is hard.

Don't believe anyone who tells you that there is only one right way to sleep train. I'm here to tell you that the "right" way is the one that guarantees both you and your child a good night's sleep.

That being said, I do have strong opinions on a few topics. Here's one.

I'm Not a Huge Fan of Co-sleeping

I meet a lot of parents (both online and in the clinic) who fell into the habit of co-sleeping, perhaps to enable breast-feeding or because of a desire to be close with their babies. When they come to me, they are now desperate to extract themselves from a pattern that essentially ensures they will sleep poorly at night. (In this book, by "co-sleeping" I usually mean a situation in which at least one parent sleeps in the same bed as the child. However, if you share a room with your child—your child sleeps in your room on a separate sleep surface such as a bassinet, crib, or bed—the interventions here will still be effective if you want to stop.)

Of course, parents who are happily co-sleeping and nursing all night long don't come to the Sleep Center, read sleep blogs, buy sleep books, or frantically Google "how to stop co-sleeping" in the middle of the night.

Here's when I think co-sleeping is OK:

- Your child is older than a year and thus the risk of SIDS is minimal.
- The family bed has enough space.
- Parents and children feel well rested in the morning and are not sleepy during the day.
- You and your partner are satisfied with the degree of intimacy you are enjoying.

If all of these circumstances are not met, then I think you should stop co-sleeping. A study in Norway supports the idea that co-sleeping can result in sleep problems down the line. The authors surveyed more than fifty-five thousand mothers and found that children who co-sleep in infancy are more likely to be poor sleepers as toddlers. Specifically, bed sharing at six months of age was associated with shorter sleep and more frequent night wakings at eighteen months of age. (If you've been co-sleeping, don't worry. You haven't caused irreparable harm to your child's sleep.) Interestingly, breast-feeding at six months did seem to result in fewer night wakings at eighteen months of age.

I understand that there is nothing sweeter than cuddling with your child during the night. Likewise, I understand that many working mothers value the closeness that breast-feeding at night provides. However, being healthy and well rested is not optional.

It's also important that you nurture your relationship with your partner. Let's be real: a restless toddler is probably going to cramp your style a bit if either of you desires intimacy. Dr. Douglas Teti, a prominent advocate of co-sleeping and the family bed, published a study showing that bed sharing after six months of age was associated with marital problems in some families: "Those who persisted with co-sleeping beyond six months tended to have higher levels of family problems. . . . The level of family chaos was higher, and the quality of care putting their baby to bed was lower."

Again, this doesn't mean that choosing to co-sleep will ruin your child's sleep or your marriage. However, if you are struggling in these areas, moving toward independent sleep will pay large dividends. It will also make it much easier to take the next steps in this book to create better sleep habits in your child.

Breaking the Feeding and Co-sleeping Habit Cycle

Since bed sharing and frequent feeding tend to travel together, parents often ask where to start. If you are in this situation, I suggest you break the co-sleeping habit now if getting your child out of your bed is a top priority. You can take on the nighttime feeds second (and I'll tell you how to do this later in the chapter). Here's why. One of the guiding principles of this book is improving your family's sleep as efficiently as possible. Practically speaking, it's almost impossible to wean if you are co-sleeping. Additionally, if you transition your child to a separate sleeping environment, this will reduce grazing at night.

Types of Co-sleeping

There are really two different types of co-sleeping: intentional and reactive. The type matters because it determines how we will approach it.

In *intentional co-sleeping*, your child sleeps in your bed or room almost every night for most of the night, and this is a long-standing pattern. In this scenario, many families want to stop once they are expecting another child, or their child hits a milestone such as kindergarten. In this scenario, you need to go gradually, because your child probably does not know another way to sleep.

With *reactive co-sleeping*, your child comes into your bed at night but in theory she is supposed to sleep in her room. This may happen most nights or even every night. *Every* family does this sometimes. I remember once when my older son, then eight years old, literally took a running jump into our bed because, he said, "I hear someone downstairs!" Lo and behold, when we got up in the morning we realized that the clothes dryer had been running all night. If your child is coming into your room on most nights for much of the night, this may resolve as you go through the steps in this book, and I would not make any changes now. If the problem persists, I recommend some interventions to try in Chapter 9.

How to Break the Co-sleeping Habit

If your child needs you in order to be able to fall asleep at night and has always stayed in your room or bed (usually via intentional co-sleeping), learning to sleep in a different room will be a *big* transition for her. If you've ever moved out of your childhood home, it can feel a bit like that. This is especially true if you are expecting another child and this is the reason for the change. There are a few steps you need to take to make this a successful transition.

- **Talk about the change.** Tell your child that you are so proud of her for becoming such a big girl, and that it is time for an exciting new step. Younger children (under two) likely can't have an extensive discussion about this, but they may still read your emotions. If you are positive and excited, they will be, too. Share your worries with your partner, not your child. Answer any questions your child has. Here are some common ones:

Q. "Can I still come into your room?"

A. "Yes, of course you can, but I think you're such a big girl that you won't need to that often."

Q. "What happens if I get scared?"

A. "Mommy is still here for you and will help you. Come get me if you are scared or sad. But I think you will like having your own space."

Q. "Is this because of the new baby?"

A. This is a tough one because frequently the answer is yes. This is why it is key to work on this well before the baby is born. I would try to encourage your child to be a good example. "Mommy wants you to work on sleeping on your own because you are such a big girl. I think that the new baby will be so proud of her big sister."

- **Make the bedroom enticing.** This isn't a bad time for a little bribery. Let your child help you pick out new sheets and blankets, or a new stuffed animal.
- **Start by moving bedtime into your child's room.** Do all of your bedtime routine (which we will refine in Part Two) in your child's room, then bring her into your room to go to sleep. Do this for three to five days before expecting her to sleep in her own room.
- **If she still naps, have her nap in her room.** Many children who co-sleep at night take naps in their own room anyway, because their parents don't have the luxury of sleeping during the day.
- **Move into her room with her for a few days.** Sleep on an air mattress next to her bed. Plan on staying in there while you work on the bedtime modifications in Part Two. Be clear, however, that this is not a permanent arrangement. For older children, tell them how long it will last, and stick to that.

Anywhere from a few days to two weeks seems reasonable. If you have difficulty exiting the bedroom at that point, follow the steps in Part Three.

If your child needs you in order to be able to fall asleep, *do not* change this part of your routine just yet. We will address this issue later (in Part Three). Many parents fail because they try to do too much at once. If your child has slept in your bed for two years and drinks four bottles of milk every night, it will be an absolute disaster if you simultaneously move her to her own room, cut off the milk supply, and expect her to sleep by herself. You will either give up (because your child is so upset and sleeping so poorly) or succeed only after weeks of tears. My goal is to minimize suffering for both you and your child.

There are a few questions that may come up in this process:

Q. What if I want to move my child out of my bed, but into a crib or bed in my room?

A. If you have the space, it is easier to have him sleep in another room. However, this isn't always an option. Using a room divider, freestanding screen, or curtain between your sleeping area and your child's can be helpful, as can a sound machine. This creates some separation.

Q. What if he shares a room with his brother or sister?

A. During this process there should not be much fussing, as you will be there to soothe your child for the sleep-to-wake transition. If your child screams every time you bring her into her room, spend a few days playing in there first, in order to create a positive association with the space. If the process is disruptive to the sibling, consider finding an alternative space for that child to sleep for a few nights.

Q. My child has never slept anywhere but my bed. How do I get him used to a crib?

A. This can be tricky. Spending time playing in the crib during the day is useful. Additionally, soothing your child to sleep and then putting him down in the crib is a good start.

The Night Feeding Habit

Years ago, I ordered a sleep test on an obese four-year-old who was waking up multiple times during the night. Since he snored, I thought it was possible that he might have obstructive sleep apnea. As it turns out, he had a different problem. The sleep study tech noted that the child was waking up every two to three hours, as the mother had told me. What she had not told me was that she was giving him an eight-ounce bottle of milk every time he woke up. Thus, we solved two mysteries—why he was waking up, and why he was obese.

Most cases aren't this extreme. Still, many families resort to nighttime feeding in order to avoid upset. But unless your child is an infant, he does not need to eat between bedtime and wake time. Nighttime feedings that persist beyond infancy aren't a necessity but a habit.

Imagine I woke you up every night at 2:00 a.m. and gave you an ice cream sundae. One week later, I stop feeding you at night—but you still wake up at the same time, hungry. This is what happens to some kids. Such "learned hunger" actually wakes you up, which is desirable from an evolutionary standpoint, but not terrific at 2:00 a.m. Like all habits, the pattern gets reinforced over time: a night awakening (cue) leads to feeding (behavior) and then back to sleep (consequence) for everyone.

This is a common habit because hunger is a powerful cue, and because the consequences of satiety and rapid sleep onset are irresistible to both kids and parents. Nursing moms and kids have the added consequences of physical closeness and breast emptying.

However, you can eliminate these habits, and doing so often rapidly improves sleep for everyone.

WHEN YOU CAN STOP FEEDING AT NIGHT

There are a few questions you need to answer before you wean at night:

- **Is your child growing well?** If the answer is no, your child may need those calories from night feedings. Some children have a condition called *failure to thrive* and require more calories that you can fit into the daytime hours. If you are not sure how your child is growing, please talk to your pediatrician.

- **How old is your child?** Bottle-fed infants typically can wean off night feeding by six months of age. Breast-fed infants tend to take longer, continuing those feedings up to a year of age. This is likely due to the fact that breast milk is absorbed more rapidly than formula. The American Academy of Pediatrics recommends exclusive breast-feeding for six months; after this, it recommends continuing breast-feeding up to a year, or longer "as desired by mother and infant."

- **Do you want to continue night nursing?** Some moms, especially those who work outside the home, value the closeness and extra time that night nursing provides. If that is the case, you don't need to stop, provided that you are getting enough rest. If not, you may need to make a choice between getting better sleep and dealing with a dwindling milk supply. If your milk supply is limited, night weaning can lead to weaning altogether. Some mothers may view this prospect with relief; others may not be ready yet.

Since these can be complex decisions, I encourage you to have a discussion with your pediatrician to figure out what is best for your family and lifestyle.

How to Break the Night Feeding Habit

There is one guiding principle here: *don't go cold turkey*. It is equivalent to asking your child to skip a meal every day. Your child could do it, but she would be miserable (and so would you). Instead, the plan is to make slow, incremental changes over time. These changes are relatively easy to make and your child should tolerate them well. The amount of time this will take depends on how many calories your child ingests at night.

The method depends on whether your child is drinking milk from a bottle or nursing. (If your child is eating tacos throughout the night, you're on your own.) Let me offer one caveat: *it is much more straightforward to wean from bottles instead of from nursing*, because with bottle-feeding you know exactly how much milk your child gets. So if you usually breast-feed, switching to bottles-only at night will make sleep training easier, even if it means you need to pump at night.

It's useful to have more than one grown-up share the burden of coming off these night feeds. If a child primarily breast-feeds at night, she often will turn up her nose when another parent shows up with a bottle at that time. This will help the process go more smoothly. If you worry that your child will cry and you will give in, it's not terrible for Mom to go away for a weekend with friends or family during the weaning process.

Note that these methods are necessary only if your child is feeding more than once at night or is taking a large volume (four ounces or more, or the equivalent via breast-feeding). Single feedings or small volumes can be discontinued rapidly.

STOP BOTTLE-FEEDING

There are two common ways to wean off the bottle, and I have a strong preference for the first one.

1. **Wean by one ounce a night.** Let's say your child takes three 4-ounce bottles a night. Take the last bottle and reduce it by 1 ounce on night one. On night two, reduce the second bottle by 1 ounce. On night three, reduce the first bottle by 1 ounce. When a bottle gets down to 2 ounces, substitute a bottle of water. After this step, you get rid of the bottle. Whatever you do, don't wake up your child if he sleeps through a feeding— that is the goal. If he skips a feeding one night but wakes up the following night for that feeding, it is OK to give him the scheduled bottle. *Pro tip:* Write this schedule out beforehand. You won't remember it in the middle of the night.

   Here's an example:

Night 1:	4 oz	4 oz	3 oz
Night 2:	4 oz	3 oz	3 oz
Night 3:	3 oz	3 oz	3 oz
Night 4:	3 oz	3 oz	2 oz
Night 5:	3 oz	2 oz	2 oz
Night 6:	2 oz	2 oz	2 oz
Night 7:	2 oz	2 oz	H_2O
Night 8:	2 oz	H_2O	H_2O
Night 9:	H_2O	H_2O	H_2O

   Limit the water bottles to 2 ounces, simply to reduce the amount of urine produced and the number of wet diapers to deal with. If your child doesn't want the water, that is fine. But don't give in and offer milk.

2. **Other ways to do this.** Two other options include increasing the amount of time between feeds or reducing calories (by diluting the milk with water) in each bottle. I don't like these

alternatives, because when you increase the amount of time between feeds, you also extend the intervals when your child is potentially crying. And when you reduce calories per bottle, it becomes too complicated to figure out how to dilute the milk from night to night. (Plus, milk + water = gross.)

STOP BREAST-FEEDING

This is a somewhat more complicated topic. For more information, I reached out to my friend and former colleague Dr. Sylvia Romm, a pediatrician and the founder of Milk on Tap, a company that provides online lactation support to families.

There are no studies on this, but from Dr. Romm's anecdotal experience, mothers find that their milk supply begins to dwindle when they start sleep training. This is especially true if they start around three or four months of age, when some mothers (especially in the United States) are going back to work full-time. This makes sense: night weaning may lead to complete weaning at this age. Alternatively, a mother can pump at night before going to sleep, or do a "dream feed" (where you don't wake up the child but feed her anyway). This might help keep up milk supply while still night weaning.

Dr. Romm suggests a few ways to night wean:

1. **Shorten each night feeding session.** This can be hard to do, however, as it is tough to be disciplined and watch the clock in the middle of the night.
2. **You can space out the feeds.** If your child feeds on a pretty regular schedule, you can try to stretch out the interval between feedings. However, this is hard to do if your kid is crying.
3. **Get Dad or the non-nursing partner involved.** This might be the most effective method. Dr. Romm says, "I've found that the

most successful method is moving the child out of the bed and picking a middle-of-the-night wake-up that's usually a feeding, but sending Dad in to the kid instead. That way the baby can be comforted back to sleep, but they learn that it's not a feeding time. Dad can't give in, so that temptation is removed. It gets Dad involved, and gives Mom more sleep. Honestly, I love daddies, but usually if the baby isn't nursed, the kiddos just start sleeping through that wake-up."

4. **Get help from a lactation consultant.** Finally, if you are continuing to struggle, please reach out to an International Board Certified Lactation Consultant, who can help you with your weaning plan and goals.

Note that options 2 and 3 are going to be pretty difficult if you are sharing a bed with your child, which is why I prefer dealing with bed sharing first.

Don't Let Tantrums Derail Your Plans

My older son had a black belt in tantrums: hard-core, day-destroying tantrums that used to last up to three hours at a stretch. They started at age three and got worse until age five, when they slowly started to improve. He's a stubborn kid. And we aggravated the situation by doing exactly the wrong thing: we panicked. We were so desperate to stop the tantrum, we tried anything and everything that worked in the moment. As I'm sure you know, it's extremely upsetting to see your child extremely upset, and the impulse to comfort him as quickly as possible is intense. Sometimes my wife and I would give in, thereby rewarding the behavior. Sometimes one of us would lose our temper, which also inadvertently reinforced his pattern of tantruming. Or we would issue a time-out, a tactic that I now know is about as effective as attempting to extinguish a fire by pouring gasoline on it. Isolating him prolonged the tantrum by ramping up his rage and frustration.

Tantrums will happen, but a bedtime tantrum can make an already stressful process feel out of control. In addition, changing behavior is like dropping a pebble into a pond: when you do that, ripples pass across the surface. So you may see an uptick of tantrums during the day as you go through the sleep-training process. Try to see these daytime tantrums as an opportunity: during the day, you may have more patience and time to work on more effective strategies for managing the behavior.

Recognize that tantrums are a habit—and that we parents need to change our own reaction to the behavior in order to help our children. Often the slightest frustration may cue an explosive tantrum. Although you may feel powerless during a full-scale meltdown, you can address this by changing your own reactions, which are the consequences that can reinforce this behavior.

Experts recommend a few different strategies for managing tantrums. The first is to reduce nagging, lecturing, and warning as much as possible, because each conflict with your child presents the possibility of triggering a tantrum. Look, I know your kids can be annoying. Mine are super-annoying sometimes. But you have to let some things slide and reserve discussion for the things that really matter. When they are singing annoying songs in the car, let them do it. When your son is throwing Matchbox cars at his brother's head, it's time to intervene.

Another is to give your child more attention in the form of physical contact. Remember, attention from you is a powerful reward for your child. Brief physical touches throughout the day (hugs, kisses, high fives, pats on the back) can help your child maintain an even keel. No need to keep track; just do it whenever you can.

Ultimately, the best way to handle tantrums isn't a time-out—

it's a *time-in*. Here's how you do it. If your child is freaking out, first acknowledge the feeling causing it ("I see you are angry because your brother took his stuffed bear from you") and then let your child know you will be with him in a few minutes when he calms down. Then ignore him until he has remained calm for two to three seconds. He needs to see you and understand that you are ignoring him and that the tantrum is not bothering you. As soon as he calms down, you can console him and give him attention. Some children will be pretty contrite at this point. Others may start screaming again, at which point you start conspicuously ignoring your child again. In a nutshell, you ignore the tantrum, give attention to the moment of calming down, and don't punish or lose your temper. Not easy, I know (oh, I know).

Once you've practiced these techniques enough, they'll start to become habit, which means they'll be more likely to kick in at times when you're more stressed or fatigued—such as bedtime or the middle of the night. And there's good evidence that just improving your child's bedtime routine by following the steps in Part Two will address bedtime tantrums as well. So be as patient as you can and continue on through the book.

ACTION ITEMS

In this chapter, we focused on changing some baseline habits to lay the groundwork for improving your child's sleep. Here are the goals you should be working toward, and how long they can take to achieve:

1. Move your child to where you want her to sleep, if she typically sleeps in your bedroom and you want her to sleep somewhere else. (This can take up to one week.)

2. Wean your child from nighttime feeds if she is older than nine to twelve months. (This can take a week or two.)

3. Manage tantrums, both during the day and at night, by changing your own habit loop.

PART TWO

THE BEDTIME CUE

A HIGH-QUALITY BEDTIME routine is the cornerstone of your child's sleep. You may already think you have a great routine, but if your child struggles with sleep, you can probably improve it. In this part of the book, I'll walk you through the perfect bedtime—where, when, and how your child goes to sleep.

Perhaps this seems like common sense. Of course you want a dark, quiet space for sleep. You definitely know that your child needs a bedtime routine. And you likely have the right timing. But parents sometimes undermine a child's sleep at night without knowing it. It's worth reexamining your child's nightly rituals, because changes are usually pretty easy to implement and can have an outsize impact on sleep.

The chapters in this part are relatively brief, and you should be able to complete them fairly quickly. Don't gloss over them, however. Developing this powerful cue—bedtime—is essential for good sleep.

One critical point: if your child needs you present for her to fall asleep, continue to help soothe her to sleep for now. We will work on transitioning your child to independent sleep in Part Three.

CHAPTER 4

LOCATION, LOCATION, LOCATION

How to Create the Ultimate Sleep Dojo

GOALS

. . . .

- Use your child's senses to make sure her bedroom is ideal for sleep.

- Learn why electronics are toxic to sleep.

- Deal with your child's nighttime fears.

WHEN I WAS A KID, my bedroom was my favorite place in the house. There was a built-in cupboard I could climb into and read, and my favorite Star Wars figures had a place of honor in the corner near my bed. I would happily go into my room at bedtime, even through high school. My bedroom was a refuge—a welcoming and safe place to play, relax, hang out, and, ideally, sleep.

This often isn't the case for my patients. Some kids scream and cry at the threshold. More commonly, kids are fine in the room—as long as Mom or Dad is there. If you are fighting with your child at bedtime or during the night, your child's relationship with his room can become fraught. This chapter will take a guided tour through your child's bedroom to make sure that it is working for and not against you. In martial arts, a dojo is a place for learning and developing strength. By following the steps in this chapter, you will make your child's bedroom the ultimate sleep dojo.

Good Bedrooms Are Dark

I see a lot of children who are afraid of the dark and prefer to go to bed with the lights on. But too much light in your child's bedroom can sabotage good sleep. (If fear of the dark is a major issue, I have some suggestions on how to deal with it later in this chapter.)

The ideal sleeping environment is really dark. I'm fine with nightlights, but here's a good rule of thumb: if your child's room is bright enough to read in, it is too bright to sleep in. Ideally, any lights in your child's room should not be in your child's line of sight—meaning that he should not be able to directly look at the bulb when his head is on the pillow. If there is a lamp on in the room, put it on the floor or behind a piece of furniture.

If your child is used to sleeping with a light on, I recommend phasing this out by putting in a dimmer switch or replacing the lightbulb in your child's room with progressively dimmer bulbs. You can perform this concurrently with the exercises later in this chapter.

Sometimes light from outside the room can be a problem as well—be it from the sunrise or from a streetlight outside his window. My younger son's wake time is definitely later when it's winter and the days are shorter. I find blackout shades or blinds to be easy and effective fixes for your child's bedroom windows, and good options can be found at local housewares stores or online. They don't have to cost a fortune—for years we used paper blackout shades from Walmart, and they worked great.

Good Bedrooms Are Quiet

My children have a superpower (and yours probably do as well): they can hear anything that I don't want them to, be it a swear word muttered under my breath or a surreptitious attempt to open a bag of candy. This is especially true regarding my alarm clock in the morning. If my alarm goes off for five seconds, my six-year-old is almost certainly getting up and coming in to see what I'm up to. This is especially true if I'm trying to sneak out of the house for an early work meeting. What is stunning about this is that he seems oblivious if I ask him to pick up his toys, even if I do it a hundred times. (My wife alleges I have a similar superpower.)

Sounds can be a major cause of awakenings, especially in the early morning. The culprits are many: the crowing of your hipster neighbor's roosters, the trash truck backing up on your street, or the guy downstairs working on mastering a kick-ass bongo solo. This is why I suggest sound masking for children's bedrooms, especially if your child is a light sleeper. White noise tends to work a lot better than music because it is much less interesting to listen to. I'm a big fan of Marpac sound conditioners, as they are almost indestructible (one of ours has been running nightly for ten years), although a fan will work just as well. I prefer that parents position these devices as far as possible from the children's ears, given some limited research that long-term exposure to loud noise at night can damage children's hearing. (According to the Centers for Disease Control, the safe level for prolonged sound exposure in infants is less than 50 decibels. Normal conversation is under 60 decibels.) You can do your own test by downloading an app that measures sound pressure at your phone and checking the sound levels in your child's room. By keeping the device at least fifteen feet from your child, you will minimize the sound exposure.

If your child shares a room with a sibling or with you, it's important to think about the effects of snoring. Loud snoring can disrupt the sleep of roommates, as well as that of the snorer himself. I recommend that all children and adults who snore regularly get evaluated by their physician.

Good Bedrooms Are Unplugged

When I started practicing as a sleep physician in 2007, the biggest battles I fought with families were over bedroom televisions. In some families, *everyone* falls asleep with the television on. It was a milestone for kids when they got a TV in their room. Parents would be offended when I asked them to take the TV out of their child's room, because they felt like I was judging them. But they would usually come around when I explained the many sleep and health issues television in the bedroom causes for kids.

- A seminal study of elementary school–age children showed that television viewing around bedtime was associated with conflict about bedtime, the tendency to fall asleep later, anxiety about falling asleep, and overall shorter sleep duration compared with children who did not watch television at bedtime.
- Teenagers who watch more TV are more likely to have sleep problems as adults.
- Preschoolers with televisions in their bedrooms are more likely to be obese. There seem to be two reasons for this. The first is that short sleep, commonly associated with bedroom televisions, is associated with obesity throughout childhood and adulthood. The second is that exposure to commercials for unhealthy foods is increased. (Let's be real—producers of

apples and Brussels sprouts aren't buying ad time on Cartoon Network at nine o'clock at night.)

Nowadays, many fewer families have TVs in their kids' rooms, but things have become a lot more complicated. It's not hard to guess why. A little device called the iPhone debuted in 2007. (A colleague recently joked that June 29—the day the first iPhone was released—will become a national holiday once we have a millennial president. At least I *think* he was joking.) Soon after, tablets (iPads, Kindles) and many other devices came along, and they have become inextricably woven into the fabric of our lives.

A study in 2015 showed that babies as young as six months of age were using mobile devices, with one in seven toddlers using them for an hour daily. This figure is almost certainly higher now. Most parents try to set limits on the use of these devices, but the lines can get a little blurry with children. What if your child is being a pain at dinner and you give him the phone so you can actually finish your beer? What if he is playing a game like Minecraft, which seems to have clear educational benefits?

Unfortunately, smartphones, tablets, and computers are more corrosive to sleep than televisions are. A review of twenty studies (assessing more than 125,000 children) showed that the use of a connected device at bedtime doubled the risk of poor sleep. There are a few reasons this is the case. First off, the light from handheld electronics is close to the eye and thus likely to suppress the body's natural secretion of melatonin. Melatonin is the signal that it is time to go to sleep, so bright light exposure wakes you up, just like caffeine (and I know you are not giving your child shots of espresso right before bed). Additionally, smartphone apps are designed to keep you using them. YouTube and Netflix both queue up the next video seconds after the one you are watching ends. Video games (even the ones for kids) layer on goal after goal, making you feel like you just need to play for five more minutes. Does this sound familiar? These apps are designed to be habit-forming by providing inconsistent positive reinforcement. Interestingly, the presence of devices seems to fragment sleep even when they are not actively in use, likely through the sounds and light from the notifications that games and social networks put out.

The real problem is our own addiction to these devices. We parents can't help checking Facebook, Twitter, or Instagram whenever we have a free moment. Like Pavlov's dog, we feel compelled to respond when our phone beeps, pings, lights up, or does something else cool.

We are also addicted to the convenience and the peace and quiet that devices provide. Younger children may pester us ceaselessly until we hand over our phone. Teenagers will retreat into the virtual and real cocoon of their rooms, phone in hand. It is easier to allow your children extra time on their iPad than to play a board game with them. YouTube and video games offer extremely useful and often irresistible bouts of free time for parents—time to work, focus, or just take a breath. I'm not saying this to make you feel guilty; I just think that we need to deploy these tools consciously. (My kids are playing a video game as I write these words.) Every parent wrestles with these issues. We have found the best balance to be no video games during the school week and a fair amount of freedom on the weekends—reducing the number of times we need to take away the devices, and the consequent friction. Even this gets blurry now that school frequently requires our kids to use Chromebooks at home.

Obviously, the reality of parenting in the twenty-first century means that you will need to make some compromises around electronics. However, I think that you need to be strict around evening and nighttime use.

Rules for Devices and Media Around Sleep

1. **No television, electronics, or electronic media for a minimum of thirty minutes prior to bedtime.** If your child gets really pumped up by his iPad (or gets super-angry when you take it away), an hour may be better.

2. **No electronics in children's bedrooms during the hours of sleep, period.** This means that you have physical custody of all smartphones, tablets, and other devices at night. It is unlikely that your child has the willpower to resist these devices if they light up the room with an alert during the night. These alerts can fragment sleep even if your child does not interact with and of the devices.

3. **Set a good example.** Don't keep your phone or your television in your bedroom. Turn your phone off when you are eating dinner, spending time with your child, or driving the car. I guarantee your children are bothered when you are paying attention to email and not them. Place your attention where it matters. In five years, you won't be sweating that email from your boss or the post you made to Instagram, but you will treasure the memory of building a pillow fort with your child.

Good Bedrooms Provide Comfortable Sensations

All of us have some sensory preferences about where we sleep. Some babies sleep better in absolute quiet. Some infants sleep better with noises, such as from a vacuum cleaner, in the background. I like to sleep on a rock-hard buckwheat pillow with the covers over my head. My wife and kids think this is absolutely ridiculous. You probably have already noticed some of your child's preferences. My older son loved being swaddled tightly as a newborn, but my younger boy could not stand it. These preferences can shift over time—my six-year-old now loves being wrapped up entirely in a sheet while he sleeps.

For most children with sleep problems, the barrier to good sleep is not physical comfort. One common (and costly) error I see parents make is buying their child a new, expensive bed or mattress, thinking this will solve their sleep problem. Many kids sleep well for years on a crib mattress. If you have ever crawled into your son's crib in a desperate attempt to soothe him to sleep (and let's be real—who hasn't?), you have noticed that those mattresses are rock hard. They have to be—this is critical for safe sleep in infancy. This doesn't mean you can't splurge on a few fun items for your child's room to help him get excited about spending time in bed. Children age two and up may be enticed by new stuffed animals or a set of sheets with their favorite character on it. Let your child pick them out, even if you think they are hideous. Most of the tired parents I know would be fine if their child's room looked like a bomb went off in there, provided their child was sleeping well.

Most children can be somewhat flexible about their preferences. However, others cannot. If your child dislikes tactile sensations such as mushy food, seams in socks, or clothing tags, he could have a sensory processing disorder. These issues are common in children with autism or attention deficit hyperactivity disorder, but they can also occur in children who otherwise do not have any developmental or medical challenges. Sensory processing disorders can affect any sensory domain, most commonly hearing, taste, or touch. Lots of people grapple with this. You may, too, if you are a person who can't stand tags on your clothing or sand in your shoes.

Sensitivity to touch (as opposed to taste or sound) is the most common sensory disorder associated with sleep problems. Some children with sensory issues do not want practically anything to touch them at night—they will sleep naked, or as close to it as possible, on top of the covers. More commonly, some children like to be bundled up tightly or pressed against you to sleep. In my clinic, there are a few bedroom interventions that have proven very helpful. (Note that these interventions are for older children—age two and up—because infants are at risk for suffocation if you use soft sheets or blankets.)

- **Weighted blankets**. These are frequently recommended because they can increase a child's sense of security. But they are expensive and very hot during the spring and summer months.
- **Lycra sheet**. A lighter-weight and more affordable option, this essentially encases your child and his mattress in a sheath, like a large sock. You can pack stuffed animals around your child to make him feel like he is being embraced. You can find such sheets on Amazon under the brand name SnugBug, or search on Etsy for them.
- **Bed tents**. These can be helpful for children who like to feel enclosed or who get overwhelmed by visual input. They are exactly what you imagine them to be—an enclosure that fits over your child's bed so that she cannot see most of the room around her. Ikea makes one, called Kura, which retails for about thirty bucks.

If you suspect your child is struggling with these issues, talk to your pediatrician about having your child evaluated by an occupational therapist.

Good Bedrooms Smell Good

Isn't it nice to crawl into bed at the end of a long day and find fresh-smelling sheets? Smell is an underused cue for bedtime. Our olfactory centers (the part of our brain concerned with smell) are among the most primitive parts of the brain. If you have ever smelled, say, your mother's perfume as you walk down the street, you know that smell can bring back memories like no other sensation. Although I do not recommend rubbing essential oils onto your child's skin (there is some evidence that these may induce hormonal changes), finding a way to incorporate pleasant and restful smells (such as a dash of lavender water on your child's pillow) may be another cue you can use to help your child's bedroom feel welcoming.

Apartment Living

Lots of sleep advice in the past presupposed that parents have the luxury of parceling out a bedroom to each child. This simply is not the case for many families. If you live in New York or San Francisco, say, or if you live with your parents, space may be at a premium. In these situations, your child may share a room with you, or with a sibling. Or perhaps you are worried that any crying at night will lead to your neighbor complaining to your landlord.

I have good news for you: it is still possible to work through the steps in this book, with some modifications. No matter your circumstances, the goal is to work on sleep training in the room where you want your child to sleep. Otherwise, you may get him sleeping the way you want him to in one space, but have to start all over again when you move him to his room. I'll give you specific examples of how to do this when necessary, but here are the general principles:

1. **Move everyone around.** A friend struggling with her younger son's sleep worried that her older son's sleep would be disrupted as she worked on sleep training in her two-bedroom apartment, where the boys shared a bedroom. Her older son was a great sleeper and very flexible. The solution was to move the older boy into his parents' room and then work on the younger boy's sleep. The older boy was excited for a sleepover, and the parents felt better knowing that he was sleeping well. You may need to move people around to get your sleepless child into his room and alone. This may even mean that parents sleep in the living room for a bit.

2. **Block sight and sound.** If you have to share a room with your child (if you live in a studio apartment, for instance), erecting barriers to sight and sound can be helpful. The easiest way to do this is with a room divider, freestanding screen, or curtain, plus a sound machine. This is especially important for young children, who sometimes have a normal awakening at night but then decide to call for Mom once they turn their head and see her there.

3. **Make a plan for noise-sensitive neighbors.** Parents have told me that their neighbors have called social services or even the police while they were doing the cry-it-out (CIO) protocol under my guidance. More commonly, you may deal with complaints to your landlord or dirty looks in the elevator. There are a couple of things you can do to avoid any unpleasantness. If you are friendly with your neighbors, explain that your child may cry during the process and ask if there is a good time (or bad time) for them. They may have a big work presentation

that week but would be fine the following week, or may even be going out of town. Bribery works, too: the gift of earplugs, a sound machine, and a bottle of wine can go a long way toward making things better. Also, some sleep-training interventions are more likely to cause crying than others. You may elect to choose interventions that are less intense but take longer, to avoid irking your neighbors.

4. **If you are moving in the next month or two, wait.** Making changes to the sleep routine may actually be much easier with a change of venue.

Note: If you are sharing a room with your child and this is your long-term arrangement (say, for longer than a month), you don't really need to make any changes right now. Remember, we will work on helping your child fall asleep by himself in Part Three.

As we move through the process outlined in this book, the majority of the interventions in Part Two can be performed whether or not your child shares a room. However, the modifications above will be helpful for some of the interventions in Part Three.

Crib-to-Bed Transition

There's one common error I see over and over in the Sleep Center. A parent says, "He cries every time I put him in his crib, so I moved him to a bed."

"How did that go?" I ask.

"Terrible! He still cries when I put him to bed. But now he follows me out of the room crying when I try to leave."

I get the logic here. Your child hates everything about being alone at night. This includes the crib. But the crib is not the problem—the bad sleep habits are. Usually, moving your child from the crib to a bed makes the sleep problems worse. Remember that you only have an illusion of control over your child's behavior. This becomes obvious when your child can wander your house at will during the night. I remember the first time I woke up and my son was standing over me staring: it was super-creepy.

Other times parents are expecting a new baby and move the older child to a new bed. I've seen this backfire if the transition occurs before age three or too close to the birth of the child. Your child is worried enough about the new baby without your taking her furniture away and giving it to the new arrival.

You can negotiate this transition successfully. Here's how:

1. **Avoid making a change before age three, or immediately before a new sibling arrives.** Remember, babies can sleep safely and comfortably in a Pack 'n Play or bassinet for the first few months of life. If you want to pass on the crib to a sibling, start the process a few months before the new baby is born.

2. **If your crib can convert to a toddler bed, convert it first before moving your child to a new bed.** Hold on to that fourth crib side and make it clear that you will put it back on if your child is struggling with sleep. Even better, keep the crib in the room and put in a separate toddler bed, with the understanding that repeated departures during the night will lead to a return to the crib. Note that you have to follow through on this if it is part of your plan.

3. **If your child can jump out of the crib, you are stuck.** I've seen children as young as eighteen months climb expertly out of their cribs. I've also known a few kids who dove headfirst out of the crib. If this is your child, you need to convert your crib to a toddler bed or just transition to a bed ASAP, even though sleep may get worse for a bit. Safety comes first. If this is the case, we will address it in Part Three.

4. **Talk up the big-kid bed.** Say to your child, "You are such a big boy now! I think that you are ready for a big-kid bed. Can you help me pick out some new sheets and blankets for you?" Start talking it up a week or two before you make a change. If your child naps, have him nap in the bed and sleep at night in the crib if you are fortunate enough to have both at the same time.

Nighttime Fears

One of the biggest barriers to transitioning to solo sleep is fear—real or imagined. Addressing this is critical to making your child feel safe in her bedroom. It can be difficult to sort out whether your child is struggling with real anxiety. Sometimes children may say that they are scared, but really they are trying to get your attention. One mother wrote me about her son's complaints:

Every night, my four-year-old comes out of his room multiple times. He will ask for a drink of water or another story. Sometimes he says there is a monster in his room and he's scared. However, he smiles when I bring him into our room and he doesn't seem particularly worried.

In this case, the little boy is expressing fear as one of many excuses for leaving his room and getting his parents. This type of behavior is known as a "curtain call," and we will address it in Part Three.

Contrast that with another child who seems to be struggling with genuine fears. According to her mother:

Our four-year-old daughter, Julia, used to be a great sleeper on her own. And then about two months ago she watched something scary on TV (totally my fault). Since then, she has had a lot of problems going to sleep by herself and putting herself back to sleep if she wakes

up in the middle of the night to go potty. As in, she cannot go to sleep
by herself—she gets super-scared and worked up, and she needs one
of us in bed with her to fall (or fall back) asleep. So that involves a
lot of waking up during the night for my husband and myself.

Nighttime fears usually become more significant after age three, when children become more sophisticated in terms of abstract thinking, and such fears may become a problem if you are transitioning your child into his own room. Sometimes you just need to provide a little bit of extra nonverbal reassurance during the day— hugs, kisses, hand-holding—to make your child feel more secure.

For children who have more intractable fears, there are some easy ways to help your child cope as you transition to independent sleep at night. Whichever intervention you choose, it's important to keep a few things in mind:

- **Avoid any scary video games, movies, or TV shows if your child is prone to nighttime fears.** Some children struggle more with this than others. My children cheerfully watched *Ghostbusters* at ages six and nine, but the first scene caused my eight-year-old nephew to throw his ice cream in the air and tear out of the room before it hit the ground.

- **If your child has a history of trauma or mental health issues, don't try these interventions without discussing it with a mental health expert.** When I see a child in the Sleep Center who suffers anxiety during the day, I encourage her family to find a local therapist, especially if the child is struggling with issues like attending school or separating from parents.

- **Be careful if you have recently adopted your child.** Many adopted children have attachment and separation issues and need expert help to address these. In either case, working with a mental health provider is the way to go.

MONSTER SPRAY

This is a simple way to help little kids who are afraid of monsters in their room at night. Get a spray bottle and fill it with water (and perhaps a tiny bit of food coloring in your child's favorite color for effect). Tell her that monsters are allergic to the spray and that it will make them sneeze, itch, and feel miserable. Ask your child to spray this in her room before bedtime—in the closet, under the bed, or any other place she would like. With time, she will use the spray less and less.

THE "HUGGY PUPPY" INTERVENTION

This intervention was originally created to help young children (ages four to six) cope with trauma experienced during wartime. Dr. Avi Sadeh, who created it, found it worked well for nighttime fears as well. Children love to help, and this taps into their best instincts to care for others. Give your child a small stuffed puppy (or other animal of your choice) and introduce them as your friend Huggy. Tell them that Huggy is usually very happy and loves to be hugged, but he is far away from home right now with no one to look after him, and this has made him feel a little sad and scared. Ask your child, "Do you think you can be Huggy's good buddy, take care of him, hug him a lot, and take him to bed with you when you go to sleep?"

After this, encourage your child to take the puppy to bed with him at night and to make him feel safe. Playing with the stuffed animal during the day can be helpful as well. It turns out that when children pretend to take care of Huggy Puppy, they become less focused on their own fears.

FLASHLIGHT TREASURE HUNTS

This is a more complex intervention for children ages four to ten who insist on having a grown-up present at bedtime because they are afraid or who insist on sleeping with the light on. If your child is really afraid of the dark, these games let her be exposed to the dark gradually, in a fun context, to help her manage her fear at night.

Get your child a small flashlight and collect a few favorite toys. Throughout the process, wait outside your child's door.

1. Hide one toy in an easy-to-find location in your child's room.
2. Turn off the lights and have her go in and find it.
3. Extravagantly praise your child's efforts to search the room alone in the dark. You can say things like, "I'm so amazed at how brave you are! You are my hero," and "I'm going to have to work harder to hide these toys because you are so good at finding them."
4. Try this a few more times (three to five) with other toys.
5. With time, increase the difficulty of the hiding places so she needs to spend more time in the dark. This treasure hunt should be brief and fun. It might take a few nights of this before she starts to feel a bit better about the dark. If your child has trouble getting started, you could try with her blindfolded with the lights on instead and have her practice finding large objects like furniture first. Depending on how things go, you may need to work up to steps 3 and 4 over several nights.

For further reading, there is a book for children called *Uncle Lightfoot, Flip That Switch*, which walks families through the process of developing a mastery of fear of the dark.

ACTION ITEMS

1. Make sure your child's room is dark, quiet, and free of electronics.

2. If you are making a major adjustment in where your child sleeps (for instance, if you are moving to a new home), talk to your child about the transition well in advance. Don't be afraid to bribe your child with sheets or blankets he picks out. I still remember the super-cool Star Wars sheets I had as a kid.

3. If you have a small living space, decide where your child will be sleeping long-term and plan where you and other family members will sleep.

4. If you are concerned about sensory issues, ask your pediatrician about seeing an occupational therapist.

5. Work on nighttime fears. Spend about a week on this while going through Part Two of this book.

CHAPTER 5

TIMING

Finding the Best Bedtime for Your Child

GOALS

- Discover the best bedtime for your child.

- Understand how late naps and your child's natural body clock can result in a difficult bedtime.

- Learn how to make sure your child is getting enough sleep.

WHEN SHOULD YOU put your child to bed? If I asked ten parents this question, they all would be sure of their answer. And the answers would vary quite a bit. Most would probably say around 8:00 p.m., but some might say 6:00 p.m. and some might say 10:00 p.m. Moreover, all of the answers could be correct, as long as the child falls asleep, stays asleep, and awakens well rested in the morning. (For the sake of clarity, by bedtime I mean the time that you turn out the lights with the intent of your child falling asleep in the next twenty minutes or so.)

For families struggling with sleep, choosing a bedtime can be less obvious. Let me share the stories of two patients I recently saw in the Sleep Center.

Jon is a five-year-old boy with problems falling asleep. He fights and argues every night from his bedtime at 7 p.m. until he falls asleep at 8:30 p.m. There are curtain calls, screams, and tears (the last from both parent and child). He sleeps through the night from 8:30 p.m. until 8:00 a.m., when he wakes up on his own.

Rob is a five-year-old boy with problems falling asleep. His parents say that they usually put him to bed at 10:00 p.m. He is very active and fidgety in the bed, and makes multiple excuses to get up and leave the room. His parents wake him up at 8:00 a.m., and he is cranky all morning.

For these families, the intervention was the same. We worked on optimizing their child's bedtime—in both these cases, 8:30 p.m. With the new bedtime, both families reported much less difficulty getting their boys to go to sleep. However, the reasons behind each intervention were different. To understand why this worked, we need to learn a little bit about the way your body decides when to fall asleep at night.

The Life-Changing Magic of Your Child's Sleep Drive

As any sleep-deprived parent or sleep scientist will tell you, sleep can be baffling. However, understanding the timing of it doesn't have to be. Once you get a sense of how this system works, it's easy to see how your child's natural sleep drive can be harnessed to make bedtime go much more smoothly.

There are two processes that work together to help determine when humans fall asleep at night. Alexander Borbély, who first described this system in 1982, called the two parts "Process S" and "Process C." We also call "Process S" the "sleep drive," "sleep pressure," or "homeostatic sleep drive." "Process C," also called the "wakefulness drive," regulates attention during the day.

Process S is pretty easy to understand. It's a signal to your body to fall asleep, and it gets stronger the longer you are awake. (A few years ago, scientists linked this to an accumulation of the neurotransmitter adenosine.) The younger you are, the faster it accumulates. That's why infants need multiple naps but six-year-olds don't nap at all. This graph shows what it looks like:

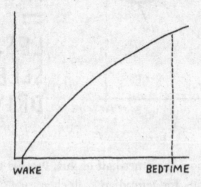

A later bedtime results in increased sleep drive. That could be one reason Jon had difficulty falling asleep at 7:00 p.m.: he wasn't tired enough.

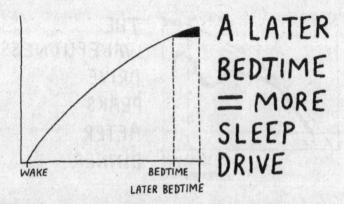

Naps can factor into bedtime difficulties as well. Long naps or late afternoon naps reduce sleep drive quite a bit. In our graph, it looks like this:

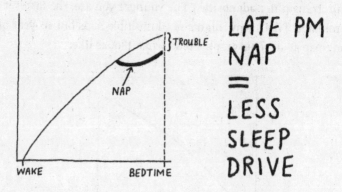

LATE PM
NAP
=
LESS
SLEEP
DRIVE

But what about the other half of this, Process C? That is a bit trickier. C stands for "circadian," which means "related to your natural body clock." You could think of it as a signal that keeps you awake as you go through the day. The ideal bedtime occurs when the wakefulness signal (Process C) is low and the sleep drive (Process S) is high:

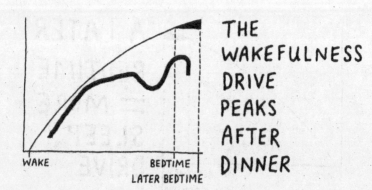

THE
WAKEFULNESS
DRIVE
PEAKS
AFTER
DINNER

Note the little valley in the wakefulness drive in the midafternoon. That corresponds to your child's afternoon nap, or the lethargy that overtakes me every day after lunch. Also note the peak at the end. That little burst explains why your child may act crazy if you keep her up after her bedtime. When parents say their kids are overtired, they are usually in this zone. Peretz Lavie, a noted sleep scientist, called this time the "forbidden zone," but I usually use the term "no-fly zone." Either way, you are unlikely to have a successful bedtime because your child is running around the house with his pants off, pretending to be a tiger. (As one parent said on my Facebook page, "My son needs to be in bed by 7:30 or he won't go to sleep until 9:00. There is nothing in between.") In this situation, an earlier bedtime *or* a later bedtime can be helpful. In kids with an inappropriately late bedtime, like our friend Rob, moving bedtime earlier can actually help quite a bit. (That he is not well rested in the morning indicates that his bedtime is too late.)

Mastering the Timing of Bedtime

So what does this mean for *your* child's bedtime?

Some children do not need a bedtime adjustment. If your child's bedtime works well, *all* of the following conditions will be met on a *typical* night:

- Your child falls asleep within twenty to thirty minutes after lights-out. (Right now, it's OK if she needs you in order for her to fall asleep. We will address this issue in Part Three.)
- There is not a lot of conflict at bedtime.
- Your child wakes up on her own between 6:00 and 8:00 a.m. and is not cranky.

If these conditions are not met, your child needs a new bedtime. The following guidelines will help lead you there:

SHOULD YOU GIVE YOUR CHILD MELATONIN?

Melatonin is a commonly used remedy for insomnia in both children and adults. Many parents of children with sleep problems have tried it on their child, and sometimes it works. But while it is often perceived as natural and thus benign, parents should keep in mind some important facts about this drug. First of all, melatonin is a hormone. I suspect most parents aren't buying estrogen or testosterone and giving it to their child without medical guidance. Second, other countries (such as the United Kingdom, the countries of the European Union, and Australia) allow it by prescription only. This ensures very precise dosing. In the United States, the FDA regulates it as a food supplement, and so producers are not subject to stringent quality control standards. A recent study showed that the amount of melatonin in a given supplement can vary anywhere from 83 percent less to 478 percent more than the labeled dose—so when you give your child a dose of what you think is 3 mg, the actual dose may be somewhere between 0.5 mg and 14 mg. Moreover, the lot-to-lot variability was as high as 465 percent—meaning that even when you buy two bottles from the same manufacturer, one bottle may have more than four times as much melatonin as the other.

Melatonin does help children sleep, however, and it may be useful in children with severe insomnia. If you are interested in trying it, please discuss the issue with your pediatrician. Making behavioral changes that will minimize the need for this medication is critical. I never recommend medication without a behavioral plan.

For more information on this topic, I have a comprehensive article here: drcraigcanapari.com/should-my-child-take-melatonin-a-guide-for-parents.

1. **The optimal bedtime for most children (up to age nine or ten) occurs between 7:30 and 8:30 p.m.** Don't believe me? Researchers studied ten thousand children at ages three, five, and seven.

They found that bedtimes later than 9:00 p.m. were associated with lower markers of future scholastic achievement, affecting in particular reading, math, and spatial abilities. The same research demonstrated similar ill effects with irregular bedtimes, meaning that a consistent time is also important for your child's development.

2. **Children should have the same bedtime most nights.** For children school-age and younger, I prefer to keep them on the plus-one schedule on weekends, meaning that your child goes to bed at most one hour later on weekends. If you let your child's schedule vary more than this, the result is equivalent to having him live in another time zone, and he will be essentially jet-lagged during the week. (Of course, your brother's wedding or similar special occasions warrant staying up later.) This can be a difficult transition. I recently spoke to a mother about her toddler's sleep problem. She and her partner had a routine of taking their child out every night for dinner with friends, and she was downcast when I said that they would need to change their lifestyle. But making that change helped the child greatly. Are there exceptions to the 7:30–8:30 p.m. window? Certainly. For instance, infants who are on a three-nap schedule (discussed later in this chapter) go down for the night around 10:00 p.m. But 7:30–8:30 p.m. is a good starting point.

3. **If your child is struggling to fall asleep at bedtime, a later bedtime may be helpful.** When the sleep scientist Monique Lebourgeois studied young children with difficulty settling at night, she measured evening melatonin levels. Although we think of melatonin as an over-the-counter remedy for insomnia, it is also a hormone that your pineal gland (at the base of your brain) makes to signal the end of the wakeful period. Normally, your body starts making melatonin about thirty minutes prior to going to bed. Dr. Lebourgeois found that

children with difficulty settling at night began secreting
melatonin at or later than their bedtime—they were being
put to sleep when their body was telling them to stay awake.
There's no easy way to measure melatonin in children outside
of research environments. However, look at your sleep diaries.
When does your child actually fall asleep on typical nights?
That time should be your child's bedtime in most cases.
For example, let's say you put your child in his crib or bed
at 7:15 p.m. and turn out the lights. He cries or fights until
8:30 p.m., at which point he actually falls asleep. Instead of
battling for an hour and a quarter every night, try moving
your child's bedtime to 8:30 p.m. I guarantee it will go easier
for you and your child, because you'll both increase his sleep
drive and likely better match his natural body clock. If you
can move your child's bedtime to the time he falls asleep and
you are within the 7:30–8:30 p.m. time frame, you are golden.

4. **If your child's bedtime is later than 9:00 p.m., this is likely because
you are on the other side of the "no-fly zone."** In this scenario,
you should experiment with moving your child's bedtime
earlier by sixty to ninety minutes. If you have a four-year-old
going to sleep at 10:00 p.m., try moving bedtime to 8:30 p.m.
This is why the exact same intervention—moving bedtime to
8:30 p.m.—can work for two children with opposite problems.
In Rob's case, his 10:00 p.m. bedtime wasn't aligned with
Process C, and his parents were trying to get him to bed
right in the middle of the no-fly zone. Once they moved up
his bedtime, he was able to fall asleep more easily. For Jon,
Process S was the issue: at his 7:30 bedtime, he had not
accumulated enough sleep drive to be able to get right to sleep.

5. **Naps should end at least four hours prior to bedtime.** If your
child naps until 5:00 p.m., you will have a hard time with

an 8:00 p.m. bedtime. (In this scenario, you can try waking your child up at 4:30 p.m. and moving bedtime to 8:30 p.m.) Watch out for what my colleague Dr. Wendy Ross calls "sneaky sleep"—those short naps in the car or the stroller back from daycare. Twenty minutes of sleep at 5:00 p.m. can cause you a world of hurt at bedtime. If you have an older child, she is often happy to volunteer to keep her sibling awake, although she may be a little overzealous. (For example, once we asked my older son to keep his baby brother awake, then noticed that he was gently prodding him with a stick he had found at the playground.)

6. **Consider your child's natural bedtime preference.** Although it's rare before puberty, some children really do have a late body clock schedule. One mother wrote me about her five-year-old son, Tommy, who would not fall asleep before 10:30 p.m. because he wanted to stay up late with his siblings. He would routinely sleep in until 9:30 a.m., but often they needed to get him up earlier—leaving him irritable during the day. Children like Tommy have a natural body clock that predisposes them to stay up later, which may become apparent if parents are not careful about setting limits—say, during summer vacation. The key to recognizing these problems is when the child wakes up. Children with body clock problems will get a normal amount of sleep when allowed to set their own schedule. I'm not talking about a single day of sleeping in after sleep deprivation. In body clock problems, the wake time, like the bedtime, consistently occurs late. In this case, Tommy would sleep about eleven hours at night if he could sleep in. If this schedule works for the whole family, it's not a problem. However, in Tommy's situation, they could not let him routinely sleep in.

In this situation, making a gradual shift to a new schedule is most helpful. For Tommy, whose mother wanted him to wake up at 8:00 a.m., his sleep period would be

Day 1: 10:15 p.m. to 9:15 a.m.
Day 2: 10:00 p.m. to 9:00 a.m.
Day 3: 9:45 p.m. to 8:45 a.m.
Day 4: 9:30 p.m. to 8:30 a.m.
Day 5: 9:15 p.m. to 8:15 a.m.
Day 6 (and all days going forward): 9:00 p.m. to 8:00 a.m.

Good sunlight exposure and exercise in the morning can also help move a schedule earlier. Finally, it is critical to maintain the wake schedule every day, as a weekend of lax bedtimes and wake times could restart the cycle of late sleeping. It also works to just start waking your child at the target time every day and putting him to bed when sleepy. This often happens with kids like Tommy when they start kindergarten.

How Much Sleep Does Your Child Need?

Remember that study of bedtime I referenced earlier with the ten thousand children, which showed that a bedtime earlier than 9:00 p.m. seemed to be associated with better school performance? Like all studies, this one had some important limitations. The biggest one was that the study did not track sleep duration. So the effect of the later bedtime on school performance may actually just reflect decreased sleep duration at night.

It can be surprisingly difficult to ascertain if your child is getting enough sleep at night. This is because children of the same age can have drastically different sleep needs. My older son needs as much sleep as or more sleep than my younger son, even though they are three years apart.

Let's review the published normal ranges of sleep, by age. Note that these are in a twenty-four-hour period and include naps:

Newborns (0–3 months): 14–17 hours
Infants (4–11 months): 12–16 hours
Toddlers (1–2 years): 11–14 hours
Preschoolers (3–5): 10–13 hours
School-age children (6–12): 9–11 hours
Teenagers (13–18): 8–10 hours

Review your child's sleep diaries. If you are using the diaries from my website, you find the typical night's sleep by counting the shaded blocks over three days and divide by three. If your child falls into her appropriate range, this is a good first step.

However, what if your two-year-old sleeps eleven hours per day (at the low end of normal)? It is still possible that she is sleep deprived. To determine this, answer these questions:

- **Does your child wake up in the morning without complaint?** It's a little-known fact that people who get enough sleep don't generally need alarm clocks. (It's little-known because sleep deprivation is so common.) School-age children and younger should generally wake up happy, bright-eyed, and excited for the day. If you need to wake your child, this implies that either she is not getting enough sleep at night (say, from an inappropriately late bedtime or prolonged awakenings at night) or she has a medical disorder that is fragmenting her sleep, such as obstructive sleep apnea or poorly controlled asthma. (If you are worried that your child is tired in spite of sufficient sleep, please review with your pediatrician the list of medical issues that can cause sleep disruption. You can find this in

Chapter 2.) One caveat here: A normal wake time for most children is between 6:00 and 8:00 a.m., especially if bedtime is between 7:30 and 8:30 p.m. If your child wakes up very early (say, 4:30–5:30 a.m.) and grumpy, this may be because of an inappropriate sleep onset association, especially if your child needs you in order for her to fall asleep and then you bring her into your room when she wakes up at 4:30 a.m. Once your child starts falling asleep on her own, this will likely improve. If not, I'll tell you how to address this in Chapter 9.

- **Does your child function well during the day compared to her peers?** In children, sleep deprivation often presents as hyperactivity, inattention, or behavioral problems. In elementary school, children may have problems performing relative to their peers.
- **Does she stay awake on short car trips around town?** I'm talking not about trips during nap time but about car rides at other times of the day. Many children will fall asleep on the three-hour drive to Grandma's house, but they should typically stay awake if you take a ten-minute drive to the grocery store. If they aren't, they probably are not getting enough sleep at night.

If the answer to all three questions is yes, you are definitely in the sweet spot and your child is getting enough sleep at night. This doesn't mean your child's sleep can't be improved (if, say, either parent isn't getting enough sleep at night, or if there is a lot of fighting around bedtime). If the answer is no to any of these questions, keep tracking your child's sleep, look for medical issues with your pediatrician, and continue to work through the techniques in this book. Remember, some short-term sleep deprivation can be helpful while working on Part Three, as your child's increased sleep drive will help her to fall asleep without you present. However, if you still worry about your child's inadequate sleep once she is falling asleep and staying asleep independently, try moving bedtime earlier by twenty to thirty minutes, as tolerated.

TOO-MUCH-TIME-IN-BED SYNDROME

Some children have a bedtime that is too early for them, but they still fall asleep quickly after lights-out. These children struggle with nighttime awakenings. This is especially common for children who had very early bedtimes in infancy (in the 6:00–6:30 p.m. range, which is recommended by Dr. Weissbluth in his book *Healthy Sleep Habits, Happy Child*). A sleep psychologist named Brett Kuhn called this the too-much-time-in-bed syndrome, and it's more common than you think. If I put you in bed at 6:00 p.m. and expected you to stay in bed until 6:00 a.m. every day, you could perhaps sleep twelve hours a night for a few days, but then you would either struggle to fall asleep or wake up during the night.

Napping: The Agony and the Ecstasy

For younger children, naps are an important part of their total sleep time during a twenty-four-hour period. Their brains are immature, and sleep helps them to grow and learn. As your child gets older, however, naps become less and less important. Sounds straightforward, right? Well, naps gave us fits with our kids and likely are causing you some pain as well.

For the first year of his life, my older son's naps were garbage. Totally terrible. If we were lucky, he would grudgingly go down for a nap after a prolonged period of fussing. Then he would be up in thirty to forty minutes, still grumpy. He was always a pretty good nighttime sleeper, especially after we sleep trained him around six months of age (see "My Sleep-Training Mistakes" in Chapter 7). But the naps remained a mess until around fourteen months. Then he really upped his nap game, going for two or three hours at a stretch. What happened? He started walking. Before then, he didn't crawl. Instead, he scooted by pulling his butt forward with his legs, a profoundly lazy and slow means of locomotion. (If you haven't seen a baby scoot and want a laugh, Google it.) Before he started walking, I don't think he was tired enough for a really satisfying nap. (My younger son napped better as a baby, but when we took away his pacifier at three years of age, he metaphorically flipped us the bird by giving up naps altogether.)

As we talked about earlier in the chapter, your child's natural sleep drive helps him fall asleep at night—the longer he is awake, the sleepier he is. The sleep drive of children increases significantly faster than yours or mine. That's why kids need naps, and we grown-ups generally don't (provided that we are well rested). But when your child falls asleep may also have to do with daytime activity, light exposure, and how recently your child was fed. It's bright outside, after all, and your child would rather hang out with you or look out the window during the day.

Naps tend to be a persistent pain point for parents because there is no clear road map for optimal napping, especially in the first year of life. The best nap timing shifts around frequently during early childhood, and the timing of these shifts occurs differently for every child. If you and your friend have one-year-old infants, there's a good chance that they both sleep at night. But one child could be napping three times a day and the other child once.

However, there are some rough guidelines to help parents find the best napping schedule for their child.

When Should Naps Occur?

As we discussed in Chapter 1, naps are troublesome because they vary so much from child to child. Let's briefly revisit how they change in the first few years of life.

Immediately after birth, your baby's schedule may not adhere to a typical day-night cycle, as we discussed in Chapter 1. Her life (and thus yours) will consist of wake-feed-sleep cycles that last for two to three hours, meaning that your child will awaken, feed, then go back to sleep again, with the cycle repeating. If it feels chaotic, that's because it is. Newborns are disorganized.

Between three and six months, most babies will start consolidating naps to longer, less frequent periods of sleeping, while transitioning to a consistent nighttime sleep period. Many children will nap three times per day, with naps occurring a few hours around awakening, around midday, and in the late afternoon. However, some kids still stick with frequent, short naps.

Sometime between six and fifteen months of age, babies taking a third nap will start to give this one up. If your infant has been in the habit of going to bed for the night around 9:00–10:00 p.m., this is the time when you can move bedtime earlier. When your child is taking two naps, the best time for naps is two to three hours after waking up in the morning and after lunch. You sometimes need to play with these times a bit to get it right, but it's good to take advantage of the mild drowsiness that occurs after a meal.

Around eighteen to twenty-four months of age, many children will transition to a single nap, usually after lunchtime, although such a transition can occur as early as fifteen months. This is when you get into the really great, long naps that actually let you get important stuff done (like paying the bills or watching an episode of *Game of Thrones*). Daytime naps usually start to drop out after age three, but some children may be ready to stop napping between ages two and three. As unimaginable as it sounds, you may choose to get rid of the nap if your child really struggles to fall asleep by 8:30 p.m.

As discussed in Chapter 1, there are a few principles to follow when dealing with your child's naps:

- **Keep it short.** Your nap time ritual should be a scaled-down version of your bedtime routine.
- **Time it right.** After six months of age, work on using the suggested nap times above, and if your child does not fall asleep after thirty minutes, get her up and wait until the next nap period.
- **Avoid napping in the late afternoon.**
- **Embrace the pain.** Nap transitions always suck. Your child does not go seamlessly from two naps to one, or one to zero. Sadly, it is not like flipping a switch. Thus, you can expect your previously angelic three-year-old to be as surly as a hungover sailor when she stops taking a nap. Avoid the sneaky sleep and try to get her to bed a bit earlier.
- **It's OK to still expect a break.** If your four-year-old no longer needs a nap, it's reasonable to expect him to have some quiet time in his room alone, especially if you need that time to do laundry, respond to email, or make a phone call.

Finally, many people struggle to establish a consistent nap and bedtime schedule for their child when there is a nanny, daycare, or preschool in the mix. Your child may nap like an angel for her nanny or preschool teacher but absolutely refuse at home. This is likely a function of the strict structure these settings have, and you should work toward similar routines (using cues and consequences, as noted earlier). Childcare settings have a few advantages that you don't. First, the cue for napping is very powerful when your child sees all the other children settling down. The second is that attention from you is much more valuable than from your child's daycare teacher or nanny. As we discuss in Chapter 7, the most powerful consequence for children is parental attention. If you aren't around, the reward for staying awake is much lower. You can't easily replicate these circumstances, but you can follow the example of many childcare centers and have very strict procedures about the timing of naps, with a very short naptime routine. Additionally, you can make yourself scarce for a set period of time even if your child is not sleeping (about thirty minutes if your child is upset). Another challenge is if your child really doesn't need to nap anymore but takes a two-hour nap at daycare every day, which destroys your hopes for a normal bedtime. I recommend you talk about this with your childcare providers to see if they have any flexibility. Perhaps your child can have quiet play during this period of time instead of a nap.

ACTION ITEMS

1. If you haven't done so already, track your child's sleep for three days and see if you are in the "sweet spot" (bedtime occurring between 7:30 and 8:30 p.m., waking up spontaneously between 6:00 and 8:00 a.m. in a good mood).

2. If bedtime is a battle, consider a slightly later bedtime, unless your child is going to sleep past 9:00; if that is the case, earlier may be better.

3. If naps are difficult, take a hard look at the timing of them and see if they fit in the typical pattern for your child's age. Recognize that naps may improve after nighttime sleep improves (or that it might be time to transition away from naps altogether).

CHAPTER 6

BEDTIME FLOW

GOALS

- Understand why a chaotic bedtime is going to short-circuit your whole night.

- Use the Bedtime Funnel to streamline your child's bedtime routine.

- Learn how to deal with pacifiers and transitional objects.

IN THE SLEEP CENTER, I often have doctors in training conduct the initial patient interview before debriefing me. Then we meet the parents and child together. Recently, a trainee, Dr. Hawkins, came in and told me about a three-year-old who was having a lot of difficulty falling asleep and staying asleep. She gave me a very detailed review of the multiple awakenings at night and all of the fighting at bedtime. Something was missing from the story.

"What about the child's bedtime? I still don't have a feeling for what they do every night," I said.

"Well, I asked them several times, but they couldn't really describe the process to me," Dr. Hawkins said.

With that, I invoked the First Canapari Rule: if parents can't tell you what they do for bedtime every night, that is the cause of their child's sleep problems. This is more common than you would think. Most families have some sort of bedtime activities in play, but they may change night to night. As we discussed in Chapter 5, it's important that bedtime occur at the same time every evening. It's also critical, however, that it contain the same activities in the same order every night. (Obviously, holidays and special occasions are an exception. But if you are making exceptions more than once a week, this likely contributes to your child's sleep difficulties.)

Fortunately, I'm going to show you how to put together the perfect kick-ass bedtime routine that will carry your child off to slumberland and support you on nights when you don't have the energy to deal. For the purposes of clarity, by "bedtime routine" I mean the activities you do every night with your child up until the moment you leave the room and turn out the lights.

The thing is, bedtime in your house is probably going to look a little different from bedtime in mine. You may have a big house or a small apartment. You might have ten kids, three dogs, two cats, and a llama, or perhaps you have an only child and are a single parent. Circumstances can vary quite a bit. But we can find a few common characteristics that the best bedtimes all share, and if you apply these principles, you will create the Bedtime Funnel:

1. Make it flow logically.
2. Create transitions from evening activities that are stimulating (such as dinnertime, vigorous play, and screen time) to calming activities and, finally, to sleep.
3. Include clear cues to prepare your child for a good night of sleep.

Let's see how these principles work together in creating the optimal bedtime. Remember, in the habit loop, you need to create strong cues to trigger the behavior you want. Previously, we determined the best time and place for delivering your bedtime cue. Now it is time to actually fine-tune that critical cue for good sleep.

The Bedtime Funnel

Your bedtime routine should help you and your child move toward sleep. Think about it as a funnel. A funnel works to channel a large volume of liquid into a small, directed stream; likewise, the Bedtime Funnel takes a large volume of unfocused energy (if your child is anything like mine) and channels it toward sleep. I've put together a set of activities that work well in sequence, though you may add or substitute others depending on priorities in your household, such as religion or a medical condition. Arrange the events so that they move your child physically closer to her bed and emotionally closer to sleep by lowering the energy level.

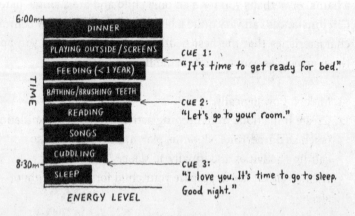

THE BEDTIME FUNNEL

6:00ᴘᴍ — DINNER
PLAYING OUTSIDE / SCREENS
CUE 1: "It's time to get ready for bed."
FEEDING (< 1 YEAR)
BATHING / BRUSHING TEETH
CUE 2: "Let's go to your room."
READING
SONGS
CUDDLING
8:30ᴘᴍ — SLEEP
CUE 3: "I love you. It's time to go to sleep. Good night."

TIME

ENERGY LEVEL

Although dinnertime is not technically part of bedtime, it's important to think about all of the evening activities that take place as your child heads toward bedtime. Dinnertime and the activities immediately afterward can be very stimulating for children, and that's OK. Some families may incorporate some screen time at this point. Limit this to no more than thirty minutes in the evening, and use your judgment about activities such as video games. (Refer back to Chapter 4 for my thoughts on bedtime and electronics.) Many children find it difficult to disengage from gaming, and asking them to do so can spark a conflict just when you want them to start calming down. If starting the bedtime routine in your home generates a lot of conflict, some experts recommend using a timer to let your child know how much longer she has to play before starting bedtime. Ideally, ask your child to set the timer as a way to participate in this process.

When you want to start the bedtime routine, *offer the first bedtime cue by saying something like, "It's time to get ready for bed."* This should be about thirty to forty-five minutes before lights-out. You don't have to use the phrase I suggested, but be very clear about what you are asking your child to do. The next set of activities can occur outside of your child's bedroom and may be a little energetic. If your child is still taking a bottle or breast-feeding in the evening, I recommend you do this outside of his room to avoid a sleep association. After this, it's time to start washing up. Not every child bathes every night, but your child likely brushes his teeth (and perhaps washes his face, if you are lucky). *Pro tip:* If you are dealing with siblings, this can be a flashpoint for conflict. As our babysitter once said, "Anytime I've ever really seen your kids fight, it's when they are brushing their teeth." (Transitions in general are hard in my home, and maybe yours as well.) The combination of tiredness and proximity can lead to some real beat-downs between my boys. If this is the case in your household, you can stagger bedtimes slightly or even have kids get ready for bed in different places.

Next, *offer the second bedtime cue: "Let's go to your room."* This prompts movement into the room where your child sleeps. This is where you do calm activities that you and your child both enjoy. Younger children may like songs before bedtime; older children tend not to. Reading has been associated with many benefits, such as improved literacy skills, closeness with parents, and creating a positive association with books and learning, so I include it as an activity for every child. If your family follows a religious tradition, this is a good time for a calm and reflective prayer. The order of activities here does not matter, *as long as they go in the same order every night.*

Finally, a quick cuddle with the lights off, and then it's time for *the final bedtime cue, which is the most important one: the signal to your child that it's time to go to sleep.* I like *"I love you. It's time to go to sleep. Good night."* If you choose to use a sound machine, this is a good time to turn it on.

The next point is critical: *if your child usually falls asleep with you present, assess whether you can leave the room without upsetting your child too much.* I suspect you know how difficult this can be, but sometimes a better bedtime routine results in an easier and more graceful exit from the child's room. If you're not sure, tell your child that you are going to step out but will come back to check on her soon. Some kids will let you leave; some won't. If you can step out of the room, terrific. Check briefly on your child in five or ten minutes. Praise her by saying, "Look what a big girl you are, lying comfortably in your bed." Give her a kiss and repeat your third cue.

If your child flips out at the prospect of your absence, don't worry. This is common if your child always falls asleep with you present. Once your new routine is established (in four or five days), try again to leave the room as described above. If you're not successful, that's OK. In Part Three, I'll show you how to use consequences to help your child achieve independent sleep with a minimum of fuss.

On the resource page on my website (https://drcraigcanapari .com/nevertoolate), you can download your own Bedtime Funnel worksheet. Fill it out and post it somewhere where it helps you keep the routine.

The Successful Flow

When you are designing your child's Bedtime Funnel, there are a few elements that will enable her to flow like water toward sleep. These will ensure that your bedtime is the ultimate cue for high-quality sleep.

First of all, *your child's bedtime needs to be concise.* If your child's bedtime drags out over hours, you create many opportunities for conflict. Look at the "lights out" time you selected in Chapter 5, and plan to clearly state the first cue, initiating your routine, thirty to forty-five minutes earlier. This should give you enough time not to feel rushed while still maintaining momentum and ensuring that your child's bedtime happens at the right time. If you continue to struggle to get your child to bed within that time frame, fine-tune the transitions between activities. Firmly but gently move your child from, say, brushing her teeth to putting on pajamas in her bedroom.

Second, *your child's bedtime needs to be linear.* All the activities, from dinnertime until bedtime, should proceed in a logical manner throughout your home. That is, each step of bedtime should move your child closer to his bedroom. If your child is running up and down the stairs ten times in the evening, he's likely getting pretty fired up and is less likely to settle down to a calm story time. Want to see what this looks like in action? Let's take the example of Zoe and Andy, a couple of five-year-olds living next door to each other.

Here's where Zoe goes at bedtime.

1. From the kitchen to the living room for TV
2. To the bathroom to brush teeth

3. To the bedroom for pajamas
4. Back to the living room for running around and wrestling with her brother
5. Back to the kitchen for a snack (spilling milk on her pajamas)
6. Back to the bathroom to brush her teeth again
7. Finally into the bedroom, where she changes pajamas as her father tries to get her to lie down for story time

By the end, everyone's heart is racing and Zoe is sweating.

Compare this with where Andy goes in the evenings:

1. From the kitchen to the living room to watch a show and then play with his brother
2. From the living room to the bathroom to take a bath and brush his teeth
3. From the bathroom to his bedroom, where he puts on pajamas, reads two stories with his dad, and goes to sleep

Who do you think has an easier time falling asleep? In my house, I will do anything to keep my kids from going back downstairs after we start brushing teeth. Any nonessential trips to, say, the living room for a book will easily delay bedtime by fifteen minutes. If your child's evening sounds like Zoe's, write down everything that happens on one night and take a look at it. How can you make it more streamlined?

Third, *your child's bedtime needs to be pleasant—for both of you.* I know this can be hard to imagine if you are fighting every night. In Chapter 4, we looked at where your child sleeps—her room needs to be a place where she wants to spend time. If she starts crying every time you bring her to her room, this is a problem. You can address this by spending some time during the day in her room doing activities she loves. Have a tea party with her stuffed animals. Make a pillow fort. Have a scavenger hunt. Read books without the pressure of a looming bedtime. If the problem continues, read the "Rehearsal" section in Chapter 8.

Finally, *your child's bedtime routine needs to be consistent.* I know I keep beating the drum about this, but it is critical to success. To paraphrase the first lines of *Anna Karenina*, all successful bedtime routines are alike; each unsuccessful bedtime routine fails in its own special way. If you create your child's Bedtime Funnel and follow it religiously every night, this powerful cue will trigger consistent high-quality sleep in your child. If your child's bedtime varies night to night, he will continue to have the same difficulties around sleep (and so will you). I encourage you to follow the same steps at least six nights per week, and reserve disruptions for special occasions such as holidays. (Obviously, after your child has been running around in the dark and eating candy on Halloween, she might have a little difficulty settling down.) Fortunately, a terrific tool can help keep you both on track: the Bedtime Chart.

The Bedtime Chart

In the bathroom of many highway rest stops and fast-food restaurants, you may notice a clipboard hanging on the wall. On the clipboard is a piece of paper with a checklist of the activities that need to be performed every time the bathroom is cleaned, along with space for the name of the cleaner and the date and time of the cleaning. There is a reason for this: following the same steps every time ensures the bathroom stays clean. The use of such checklists is widespread in many industries: You'll find them in the operating room of your hospital. Pilots use them before they even think about flying the plane. A Bedtime Chart simply takes advantage of this powerful tool.

A Bedtime Chart depicts your child's bedtime routine. (To avoid making it overwhelming, limit it to three to five activities.) If you enjoy crafts with your child, spend as much time designing it as you like, but you don't have to go crazy. One father showed me a Post-it on which he'd drawn a toothbrush, a book, and a bed. Every night his two-year-old would point to each step before she would do it.

For children who can't read, you might glue pictures or objects to the chart for each step. You could glue an actual toothbrush, a picture of your child brushing her teeth, or a picture of a child brushing her teeth from a magazine. If your child has to take medication (say, an asthma inhaler), put that on your chart. Some recommend including a "one last thing" element for children who tend to stall, such as one extra hug after lights-out. This doesn't need to be a checklist, but if your child likes checking boxes, go for it.

If your child has ADHD or autism, these charts can be especially helpful. Children with autism may benefit from having a physical object (imagine a toothbrush, a set of doll's pajamas, a book, and a dollhouse bed), attached to a strip of Velcro, that they pull off and put in a bin when the task is completed.

You can also use the Bedtime Chart to create a reward system. I recommend pasting photos to a whiteboard and creating a grid that allows a box to be checked each day of the week. I have some examples on my website at https://drcraigcanapari.com/nevertoolate. For more on using rewards, please refer to Chapter 8.

Blankets, Binkies, and Bears, Oh My

When my older son was born, my wife's boss sent us a gift basket with monogrammed towels, blankets, and a single small teddy bear. This was added to the collection of about thirty stuffed animals he had been given up to and around his birth. It was a small soft bear with a blue ribbon tied around its neck. Really, there was nothing remarkable about it, except for one thing: my son has been sleeping with it nightly since around one year of age.

This teddy bear (imaginatively named "Bear") has been my son's constant companion since then. I cannot entirely explain the complex alchemy that led to this being the object of my son's affection. I do know that if there was a fire, Bear is one of the first items I would grab when evacuating my family. We double- and triple-check if we have Bear when we leave for vacations. Now that he's a bit older, my boy won't bring him on sleepovers with friends, but otherwise he sleeps with Bear nightly.

Beloved objects such as Bear are known in the medical literature as "transitional objects." Stuffed animals and blankets are common transitional objects and can help children move to independent sleep. My niece has a beloved rubber rat she sleeps with, called "Baby Rat"; her parents are less fond of it than we are of Bear.

Not every child will be interested in a transitional object. When we tried to encourage my younger boy to bond with this or that toy, he would obligingly hug it, then chuck it out of his crib when the lights went out. However, you may have better luck with your child, and it is worth a try if your child is anxious at bedtime. *Note that it is not recommended that children under the age of one year sleep with any soft objects (loose blankets, stuffed animals, etc.) because of the risk of suffocation.*

It's easiest to introduce a transitional object if your child is younger (say, one to three years). If your child has a favorite stuffed animal, that's great. Otherwise, ask her to pick one to help her with bedtime. (This can be especially useful if your child has nighttime fears—for more information, check out the "Huggy Puppy" intervention on page 94 in Chapter 4.) A knotted T-shirt that smells like Mom or Dad can work just as well. Have your child hold her object during bedtime and take it into bed with her. Don't force it, though, if your child isn't interested. When you start transitioning toward independent sleep in Part Three, ask your child to take good care of it during the night.

Pacifiers (also known as binkies, or dummies in the United Kingdom) are another type of transitional object. I bet you are familiar with them. Some kids love them and some kids don't. I loved the magic effect of putting one in the mouth of my crying babies and having them fall asleep. The American Academy of Pediatrics recommends offering a pacifier at nap time and bedtime in the first six months of life, as using one confers a slightly decreased risk of SIDS, even if the pacifier falls out of your child's mouth. From a behavioral standpoint, I have found that you have two windows for getting rid of your child's pacifier with a minimum of fuss. The first is around six to nine months of age. The second is usually around age three—and after three, use of a pacifier can affect your child's teeth. I always thought we would get rid of our kids' pacifier in the first window, but my wife wanted to wait until later. So both of my boys received a visit from the Binky Fairy: after discussing the fact that "the babies are going to need your binkies now that you are a big boy," we packaged them up and left them outside their room. That night, after our children had gone to sleep, we removed the package and placed a small gift in its place.

You may need to think about getting rid of the binky sooner if it creates a sleep onset association disorder for your child. If you need to breathlessly race in multiple times a night to reinsert it in your child's mouth (or if your child is throwing it out of her crib at night and demanding her parents come in and get it, as my niece did), it is probably time to get rid of it. Remove it at bedtime as part of the consequence technique you choose in Chapter 8.

Questions and Answers About Bedtime

Obviously, every family is going to have to create a routine that works well in their home. Here are some questions that often come up.

Q. Who should do bedtime?

A. Just as with infants, it is important that all of the caregivers in the home be able to help a child to transition from wake time through bedtime into sleep. Unfortunately, I hear the same refrain from tired parents that "my son will only go to sleep for me" (and in heterosexual relationships, it is usually Mom and not Dad who is carrying this burden, unfortunately). As we talked about in Chapter 1, it's critical that your child be able to go through his routine with each parent. If your child has never learned to do so with one parent, it's time now. The best way to do this is to have Mom go out of town for a few days (preferably to a cave underground with no cell service, although a weekend away with friends will usually do). Trust me, Dad and child will figure it out. If discussing this with your partner stresses you out, here's what to say: "We've been struggling with Ryan's sleep for a while and I don't think I can fix it on my own. I need you to take over bedtime some of the time so that he can start sleeping more independently."

Q. What if my child nurses to sleep?

A. This is an issue often seen with younger children and is one of the most common sleep onset associations. After about eight or nine months of age, however, nursing to sleep (versus nursing thirty minutes earlier) is not going to make the difference between sleeping through the night or awakening to feed. The best thing to do now is to move nursing earlier in the bedtime sequence.

This is going to feel strange if nursing to sleep is the only way you've done it for your child's entire life. Here's how I recommend approaching it:

1. Nurse your child first thing in the bedtime routine, preferably outside of her room.
2. If possible, have another caregiver take over bedtime after this (see "Who should do bedtime?" for why).

There may be some tears, but it is OK to stay with your child and soothe her to sleep at this point, if necessary.

Q. What if my child starts crying after I change his routine?

A. Although some of the changes we've discussed in this part may seem drastic, often they go very smoothly. If your child fusses a bit, do your best to provide gentle reassurance, but try to exit the room as quickly as possible. If he starts crying more, it's OK to go in and soothe him back to sleep. We'll talk about how to remove your involvement in Part Three.

Q. What if my child won't fall asleep unless I'm present?

A. In this part, we've worked toward perfecting your child's bedtime routine to make it the best possible cue for high-quality sleep. If you feel like your child still needs you in order for her to fall asleep, that's OK. Continue what you are doing to help her fall asleep for a week or two while you review the materials in Part Three. It's totally fine to keep her company for the time being. Some kids learn to sleep better with the interventions we've performed so far. If you are still unsatisfied with your child's sleep, we will work in Part Three on using consequences to ensure that the whole family is getting a good night's rest.

ACTION ITEMS

1. Fill out your Bedtime Funnel worksheet (available at https://drcraigcanapari.com/nevertoolate). It's fine if you end up with a bedtime routine that looks much the way it did before. Many families will. But systematizing this will help you provide a consistent cue every night. It's especially important to decide on the verbal cues you will be using every night.

2. Make a Bedtime Chart. The Bedtime Funnel worksheet is a reminder for you; the Bedtime Chart is a reminder for your child. Pictures work great, as do simple words for children who can read. You can use a whiteboard if you want to have your child check a box at each step. (Personally, I love checking boxes.)

3. Live with your new routine for a week or two. It's time to implement this routine at the new bedtime in your child's fully optimized sleep dojo. For some kids, this is all that you need to do. So if things aren't perfect, just wait a bit. If you still need to improve your child's sleep, move on to the next part of the book.

1

PART THREE

THE TRUTH ABOUT CONSEQUENCES

BY NOW, YOU should have completed the following steps: You've cleared major obstacles by stopping night feedings and moving your child to her own room, and you've worked during the day on overcoming fear of the dark and tantrums. You have also established a kick-ass, perfectly timed bedtime routine. Pat yourself on the back, as you have laid the foundation for a lifetime of good sleep for your child.

By now, either your child has started falling asleep on her own, sleeping through the night, and getting up at a reasonable hour in the morning, or—as is very common—your child still needs you to be present to fall asleep and is continuing to wake up at night or too early in the morning.

If you've arrived at the first scenario, congratulations! It really can happen, and I hope it has happened for you.

If you haven't yet, don't lose hope! We are going to use the other part of the habit loop, consequences, to move your child to independent sleep.

CHAPTER 7

THE SOLUTION BEGINS WITH YOU

GOALS

· ·

- Revisit the way *your* behavior powers your child's sleep habits.

- Know why sleep training is safe.

- Understand why you will succeed even if you have failed before.

ONCE YOU REFINE BEDTIME, we've reached the home stretch—
even if your child isn't yet sleeping independently.

Why is it important to get your child to fall asleep on his own?
Because if your child needs you to be present for him to fall asleep
at bedtime (that is, your child has a sleep onset association disorder,
described in Chapter 2), he will need you to go back to sleep in the
middle of the night. He has learned to associate your presence with
the ability to sleep. Exiting the room before your child falls asleep
usually results in fewer nighttime awakenings within a few weeks.
(If your child is falling asleep independently but is still having troublesome awakenings at night, I encourage you to read this chapter
before skipping ahead to Chapter 9.)

Sounds easy, right? If you've tried sleep training before, though, you know this is the hard part.

In this chapter, I want to teach you how to become a parenting ninja by mastering the art of managing your own behavior. Accomplishing this will help your child sleep better. More important is that, as a ninja, you will be able to reshape your child's behavior *without him even noticing*.

Why Your Behavior Is So Important

Let's go back to the habit loop we discussed in Chapter 2 and look at what happens when your child is not used to falling asleep on her own. When you leave the room, this gives her a cue to start crying, or arguing, or delaying. Like many tired parents, you relent—you go back in and stay with her until she falls asleep.

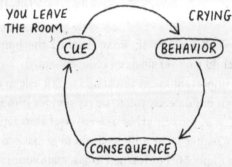

Recognize that this is another example of a double habit loop. Your tired brain has been conditioned to have you go back in to get her to sleep as quickly as possible. Here's how that works:

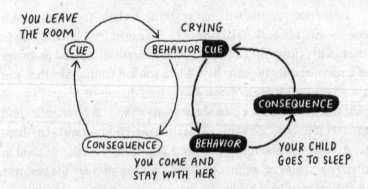

In this case, your child's protest cues your acquiescence to her demands—*your* behavior, so that you get the sweet, sweet nectar of that child-free time. And the two loops continue to roll on every night, both at bedtime and in the middle of the night when your child has natural awakenings.

As you can see, your child's consequence and your behavior—your reaction to *her* behavior—are one and the same. Changing the consequence without changing your own behavior would be pretty tough. Here's an email I got from a parent who is trapped in exactly this double habit loop:

My husband and I sleep trained our five-year-old with the assistance of an in-home sleep trainer when he was an infant. For the past two or three weeks, sleep has tanked in our home and we can't identify what the hiccup is . . . and we've made it worse with rubbing backs, "come in our bed," etc. We are now two weeks out from using all of our learned techniques and he still wakes seemingly terrified. If we don't intervene, he suffers and wakes up his brother and sister. It's affecting their behaviors at school and they are tired. He is starting kindergarten in three weeks and we want to start the year right.

Desperate parents will try anything to help their child calm down—rub his back, take him into their own bed, hunt for monsters in the closet with a flashlight, even make whispered promises of a new Lego set the next day. When you are flailing like this, you are powering a habit loop you don't want: disrupted sleep. To avoid this, you need to have a plan about what you will do when your child thwarts your best-laid plans. (And trust me, children will.) In Chapter 8, we'll talk about specific strategies. First, though, we need to understand how consequences work, and why they are the best way to change your own habits and create new ones for your child.

In Part Two, we talked about the bedtime routine—the ultimate cue for a night of high-quality sleep. We started there because it really works. It also occurs at a time when parents have more energy compared with, say, the middle of the night. This is also where we will focus on adjusting consequences. We need to interrupt the part of the loop that is *your* behavior (and your child's consequence). Here is where we will focus our sleep-training intervention: after your child's undesirable behavior. To do so successfully, you need to have a plan for what to do when this behavior triggers *your* habit loop.

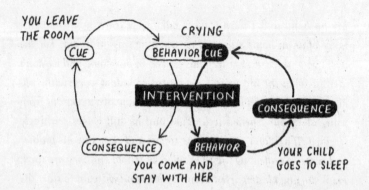

The Power of Consequences

I want to focus here on the two most effective types of consequences: positive consequences and extinction.

You can't directly change your young child's behavior by issuing instructions, commands, or heartfelt pleas. If she wants to draw on the walls with a Sharpie, she will find a way to do it. But you can definitely change how you react. You can, for example, raise your voice, grab her markers, and take away her teddy bear. These are negative consequences—what we call punishment. But negative consequences aren't very effective; in fact, they often backfire, causing your daughter to repeat the behavior in question when she wants your attention. (Think about it—a major freak-out from you lets her know that acting out is a powerful behavior guaranteed to get attention.) Children, especially bored or anxious ones, often desire any kind of attention from Mom or Dad. This is why your kids often interrupt you while you are composing an email or talking on the phone. They would rather you acknowledge them even if it means yelling.

The other thing about negative consequences is that dishing them out doesn't feel very good to us parents. Responding in anger will lead to guilt and regret. Still, know that your child is resilient, and that you likely haven't harmed him. You haven't ruined his long-term chances for happiness or your chances for a good night's sleep. Try to forgive yourself, and set to work on making the situation better.

What else can you do besides losing it with your young artist after she has created a primitivist masterpiece on your wall? You can explain to her (after taking a deep breath) why drawing on the wall is a bad idea, get her a piece of paper, and sit her down at the kitchen table with a snack and a kiss (positive consequences). By rewarding the behavior you want, you hack the habit loop—you've changed your behavior to create a better consequence for your child.

Sometimes the most powerful option is looking the other way—a subtle but effective attention-based equivalent of a time-out. (The unfortunate behavioral term for ignoring undesirable behavior is, again, "extinction.") Of course, this may not be an option when your daughter is doodling all over your walls, but there are plenty of other opportunities when your best option is to do nothing at all. Does your son insist on speaking in a funny voice at the dinner table? Ignore him. Does your daughter always interrupt you when you are taking a work call? Walk into another room and calmly close the door. Does your child amusingly use farts as a punch line? Do your best not to laugh (and if you figure out how to do this, let me know). The most famous sleep-training method in the world, popularized by Dr. Ferber, is a modified extinction program. One thing to remember is that extinction methods often result in a brief flare of the problem behavior (that's the extinction burst I mentioned earlier).

Here is the key point to remember: *If your child is doing something over and over that you want to stop, focus on your reaction to the behavior. Your reaction powers the habit loop.*

My Sleep-Training Mistakes

As I mentioned back in Chapter 1, when my older son was six months of age, I thought I had it all figured out. He had been sleeping through the night for about a month, without any alteration of our classic first-child bedtime routine. My wife and I would bathe him together, put his pajamas on together, and read him a story. My wife would nurse him to sleep, and then she would pass him to me and I would gently lay him down in his crib. Then one night he woke up and needed to be fed. The next night, he woke up twice.

The third night, three times. It took about a week of waiting for the problem to go away on its own (which it didn't) for me to realize that we had missed our chance to easily transition to independent sleep (as described in Chapter 1).

Like most pediatricians, I elected to use the cry-it-out, or CIO, method (as I'll explain in Chapter 8, it's the most direct method). We abruptly switched from nursing him to sleep to putting him into bed drowsy but awake. And it was terrible. The first night, he cried for about an hour. We tried checking, but it was like putting gasoline on the fire. The next night, we decided to just let him cry until he fell asleep. This lasted for two and a half hours. My wife was in tears. It was awful.

The next night, he cried for twenty minutes. By the fourth night we were done—he was falling asleep independently and the awakenings resolved in a few days. But it was not fun.

There are a few things I wish I had done differently. The first is that we missed his cues that he was ready for independent sleep—that he was naturally sleeping for longer periods, and then that he began to wake at night again. The second is that we did not try to fine-tune his bedtime or use a temporary later bedtime (called "bedtime fading" and discussed in Chapter 8). This would likely have made the process easier. Finally, I wish I had sent my wife out with friends that second night. As a pediatrician, I had dealt with a lot of crying, but for her it was more painful. (Not that it was easy for me.) This is a common pitfall that can be circumvented if you have a frank conversation with your partner before any behavior change program. If we had discussed it in advance, we could have planned to avoid a difficult evening.

SLEEP TRAINING IS SAFE

Since we are talking about Dr. Ferber, let's talk about the safety of sleep train-ing. Sleep training doesn't just mean the method popularized by Dr. Ferber, which is technically called "graduated extinction" ("graduated" because it involves parents checking on the child at increasing intervals, "extinction" because it involves ignoring the child's demands) and commonly known as "cry-it-out", or CIO. However, it is perhaps the most well-known method of sleep training, and, as we discussed in Chapter 3, it is controversial.

Extinction-based sleep-training methods are very effective, and many studies have shown that they are safe. However, these methods have been nicknamed "cry-it-out" for a reason, and parents often find it difficult to toler-ate stretches of crying. Also, as noted earlier, some proponents of attach-ment parenting allege that it causes brain damage in children.

So what about sleep training in healthy children? What's the evidence that it is safe? Well, there is no evidence of any harm to children across mul-tiple studies of thousands of children. Most of the studies on this have looked at CIO, as this is the most controversial method, but other methods have been examined as well. The best long-term study was performed by a group in Australia led by the psychologist Dr. Harriet Hiscock. The Kids Sleep Study followed 326 children for the first six years of life. Families in the study had been offered either sleep-training guidance or routine care. The authors reported that children who had sleep trained via any method in infancy slept better at two years of age and their mothers were less likely to be depressed. Several years later, the researchers looked at these children again and noted that there was no evidence of emotional or behavioral problems in children who had sleep trained versus those who had not. They also measured the stress hormone cortisol, which is frequently cited by opponents of sleep training as the mechanism by which crying causes problems for developing brains. The researchers did not find any evidence of differences in cortisol secretion between children who had sleep trained and those who had not. Thus, these children did not show any evidence of increased stress responses in later childhood.

I found these results to be tremendously helpful. First off, they provided long-term evidence of the safety of sleep training. Second, they acknowledge that most kids sleep better with time, no matter what you do. This is a very parent-positive finding, and one that reflects the philosophy of this book. There is so much pressure on all of us, particularly via social media, to be perfect parents—to enroll our toddler in Mandarin classes, put her down for Hogwarts, breast-feed her until kindergarten, and choose the optimal parenting strategy for every challenge. But you don't have to be a perfect parent. As a famous pediatrician and psychoanalyst named Donald Winnicott said, children just need a "good-enough mother"—a mother (or father) who loves her child and does her best to take care of him. Likewise, my goal for you is "good-enough sleep"—because nothing is ever perfect, but everyone in your home needs to be sleeping well enough to be in a good mood, function well, and be safe behind the wheel.

Discovering the "Positive Opposite"

Dr. Alan Kazdin, a behavioral psychologist at Yale whom I mentioned back in Chapter 2, has made a lifelong study of the use of habit psychology in shaping the behavior of children. He talks about encouraging the "positive opposite" of the behavior you want to change, which is simply how you would like your child to act. To do so, you need to imagine what that looks like. It's probably not hard to imagine if you are struggling with your child's sleep. Your positive opposite likely includes his falling asleep, staying asleep, and waking up at a decent hour in the morning.

In moving your child toward the positive opposite, your most effective tool for making long-term change is providing positive attention and praise. Often we parents react to bad behavior but ignore good behavior. When my son freaks out ten minutes before dinner because he wants a snack, I either give him one or yell at him. But if he is sitting quietly and playing a board game with his brother, I sigh with relief and finish cooking dinner. Don't miss opportunities to praise your child for doing a good job. Notice any small steps toward that perfect night of sleep. If your child fights less at bedtime, praise that. If your child stays in his room ten minutes later in the morning, give some extra hugs and kisses. If you want your praise to work, it should be lavish and over the top— think shows for kids like *The Wiggles* or *Barney*, even if you roll your eyes at the way the performers act.

Remember that things won't improve overnight. Praise small steps like they are big victories. Err on the side of praise even when things aren't perfect or when there is a step back. Finally, praise things your child *can* control—and don't chide her for things she *can't*. Your child can lie in bed, but she can't control when she falls asleep. She can be brave when she is scared, but she can't control whether or not she is afraid. She can't control if she wakes up at night; she can control how she handles it. We will talk in Chapter 8 about reward systems for older children and also discuss Dr. Kazdin's work a bit more then. If you are on the fence about your child meeting the goals you set for a reward, always give her the benefit of the doubt and round up—that is, reward her for a good try.

Keeping the Peace: Coming Up with a Plan Everyone Can Live With
Changing behavior is hard, especially when it involves not only changing your own and your child's but your spouse's as well. Everyone in your home must agree about what you plan to do.

There are a few questions I recommend you discuss to help guide your choice of a sleep-training method.

- **Are my partner and I in accord on this?** It's OK to have misgivings, but you have to agree to the plan and commit to its success. There's an episode of the TV show *Modern Family* where two parents get into a wrestling match on the floor of their child's room after one rushes in to stop their daughter crying and the other tries to prevent him from doing so. Don't discover halfway through the process that one parent really objects to a particular method of sleep training.
- **Is one parent going to have a harder time than the other?** As a pediatrician, I had developed a great deal of tolerance for the crying of children, but my wife really suffered. Be honest: if one parent needs to leave the room (or even the house) for the plan to be successful, do it. Use each other's strengths.
- **Can we endure listening to our child cry for several hours on the first few nights?** This is the big one for CIO. You can expect improvement within a week, but the first few nights can be difficult. This isn't for everyone, and that's OK. In the next chapter, I offer several methods that may take longer but reduce the likelihood of crying—these might work better for you.
- **Can we offer our child a choice?** When you look through the options for helping older children, one or two may be your favorites. If your child is preschool age or older, it may be worth presenting the options to your child as well. Make sure you talk in age-appropriate language. Often it is good to present it as a game, especially for rehearsal techniques (discussed in Chapter 8). But only offer options when you can live with either choice. Think "Would you like the chicken or

the fish?" and not "Would you like to be in a scary dark room by yourself or to sleep in my bed until you go to college?"

But We Tried and Failed at Sleep Training Before, So What's Different?

This chapter has been about the theory of using consequences to improve your child's sleep. Chapter 8 will give you concrete strategies to put this theory into practice.

Many of these strategies are part of what most people would consider "sleep training." While much of what we've done so far doesn't fit into the standard perception of sleep training, it does involve a deliberate effort to encourage better sleep through behavioral change techniques. That includes creating a better bedtime, which acts as a positive sleep cue; even if you haven't seen the benefits of these changes yet, the next steps (changing the consequence) will be much easier.

When it comes to consequences, positive reinforcement (rewards for good behavior) and extinction (ignoring behaviors you don't like) outperform negative reinforcement every time. Ferber's method is a classic example of changing consequences to shape behavior. By leveraging consequences, we will get you and your child to better sleep and a better life. Remember: establishing a positive sleep cue through bedtime will make your sleep-training techniques much more effective than they've been in the past. Not easy, necessarily, because being a parent is hard, but definitely much easier since you will already have primed or cued your child for sleep.

Whatever technique you choose in the next chapter, you will have more success if you recognize a few truths: your child's behavior will not be perfect—and neither will yours. You need to be patient and compassionate, starting with yourself. I don't know a parent who hasn't screamed at his kid for a trivial matter and immediately regretted it. I also haven't met a perfectly behaved child. Children test their limits to understand their place in the world. Your job as a parent is to help them find it.

ACTION ITEMS

1. The next time your child does something that annoys you, take a moment and pause. What is your instinctual reaction? Would the consequence lead to the annoying behavior happening again?

2. Identify the consequences that you provide (at bedtime or in the middle of the night) that may prevent your child from sleeping independently through the night.

3. Discuss with your partner (and with your child, if she is old enough) what would be the best fit for your family.

CHAPTER 8

CHOOSING YOUR CONSEQUENCES

GOALS

• Review the different sleep-training techniques available for you and your child.

• Pick one and get started.

• Consider a slightly later bedtime to start.

YOU'VE WORKED HARD to create the perfect bedtime routine for your child, but things still aren't perfect. Perhaps she still needs your presence to fall asleep, or she wakes up five times per night. Maybe she gets up way too early as well. (If she falls asleep and stays asleep on her own but still has persistent early morning awakenings, go straight to Chapter 9.) In Chapter 7, we talked about the general principles of consequences—how you will use these techniques to manage your own response to your child's behavior in order to change her habit loop.

In this chapter, I'm going to walk you through my favorite sleep-training techniques. I'm including a diversity of approaches so you can find one that fits your circumstances and your parenting style.

The goal of any of these techniques is achieving independent sleep for your child at bedtime.

I've divided up these interventions by age and venue of sleeping. For most kids these will overlap. So "crib" interventions will work best for kids between six months and two to three years of age. "Bed" interventions are aimed at kids from two and a half to three years and up. Many of the "bed" interventions will work well for children through elementary school as well.

One thing is critically important: *don't start here if you have skipped Part Two*. The methods described here (consequences, the third part of the habit loop) are much less effective if you don't have a great cue (the first part of the habit loop)—specifically, a bedtime that is calibrated for your child and family. Many families I see in the Sleep Center have tried and failed to sleep train because they did not work on bedtime first. When I see them, we adjust bedtime *first* and then get the results they desire. So do yourself a favor and make sure you've carefully read and followed the suggestions in Part Two.

There are a few other rules to remember for success:

1. **Pick an intervention and stick to it.** Find something that feels right for you and your family and try it for at least two weeks. This also means starting when you have two weeks without any major anticipated changes to your child's routine (trips, relatives visiting, etc.).

2. **Keep a daily sleep diary so you can measure your progress.** Progress is often subtle in the beginning. Also, please fill these sleep diaries out in the morning! The last thing I want tired parents to do is middle-of-the-night homework. You can download these diaries from my website at https://drcraigcanapari.com /nevertoolate.

3. **Be very consistent.** Remember, changing habits is hard, both

for you and for your child. Commit to following through on your plan for at least a few weeks (ideally a month) so that you can get through any extinction bursts. New habits need up to a month to take hold.

4. **Decide in advance how you will deal with nighttime awakenings during your sleep period.** I encourage you to repeat the bedtime intervention if your child quickly awakens after falling asleep. For example, if you put your child to sleep at 8:00 p.m. and he wakes up at 9:30 p.m., repeat your intervention. For awakenings that occur during the time when you are usually asleep, there are two strategies, both valid.

   a. You soothe your child back to sleep if he wakes up. This is likely the best solution for most families, as it preserves parental sleep while letting the bedtime cue-and-consequence approach create the habit of independent sleep over several weeks. I especially like this approach for longer-time-frame interventions (such as "camping out," discussed later in this chapter) or single parents who don't have the luxury of dividing nights into shifts with a partner. Awakenings should improve in a few weeks once your child achieves independent sleep at bedtime.

   b. You apply your consequence plan if your child wakes up. This is a better fit for interventions that work more quickly, such as cry-it-out. If you are doing CIO, do a quick check, then leave the room. If you are using the progressive breaks method (discussed later in this chapter), you repeat bedtime.

A REMINDER ON TIMING

In Chapter 5, we talked about the best time for your child to go to sleep. For most kids, this will likely be between 7:30 and 8:30 p.m. As you go through the consequences in this chapter, you may find that your child is staying up later or even skipping naps (the dreaded "nap strike"). This can be exaggerated in younger children during a CIO-based intervention. You will be tempted to allow your child to sleep in the next day or get extra sleep during the day, including "sneaky sleep" in the car or stroller. A ten-minute nap in the car on the ride home from daycare in the late afternoon can short-circuit your plans at bedtime. (If your child has an older sibling, she may be more than happy to keep your young one awake.) You need to avoid this, even if your child is really cranky for a few days. This irritability is actually a good sign, as it means that your child has increased sleep drive and will be sleepier and sleepier at bedtime as you move through this process.

Likewise, if you let your child sleep in, he will be less tired at bedtime; worse, it may have the unintended side effect of allowing his natural sleep period to move later. This can be desirable if one of your issues is persistent early awakenings, but don't allow your child to sleep later than 7:00 or 7:30 a.m.

One intervention that *can* be helpful is a slightly later bedtime. Again, this will harness your child's natural sleep drive to help him fall asleep more easily. If your child's bedtime is usually at 8:00 p.m. and he is not falling asleep until 9:00 p.m. under the new regime, a temporary bedtime of 9:00 p.m. may help him transition more quickly to independent sleep. Once he is falling asleep within fifteen minutes of lights-out, you can move his bedtime earlier by ten minutes every day or two to get back to your usual bedtime.

Techniques for the Crib Sleeper

These techniques are targeted to younger children, from about six months to three years. There are really two techniques: CIO (and its variants) and the "camping out" method. Even if you've tried CIO and failed in the past, don't rule it out. If you've followed the plan in Part Two to create a better bedtime, it might work really well. "Camping out" works better for families who want to avoid crying, but it can have its own difficulties. Read on for the details of each approach.

Cry-It-Out and Variants
Time to better sleep: Quick
Stress level: High
Best age range: Six months to two years, although you can do it in older children provided they are in a crib

Cry-it-out (also known as extinction) is the great-granddaddy of sleep-training techniques. As discussed earlier, it has been controversial, but the best evidence available suggests that it is safe. It is simply defined as the withdrawal of parental attention from behavior you don't like—specifically, the need for your child to have you present when she falls asleep.

The prospect of leaving your child crying in the dark and not comforting her is hard to imagine. Many parents who try this give up very quickly, and for good reason. We are hardwired to respond to our child's needs from birth. Scientists have shown that mammal infants who lose the ability to cry are ignored by their mothers and eventually die. Likewise, research on neurosurgery patients showed that a recording of an infant's cry caused a rapid response in a part of the brain associated with urgent, do-or-die behaviors twice as fast as other recordings. However, unlike our ancestors thousands of years ago, we don't live on the African savanna, where a crying child might prompt an attack from a saber-toothed tiger. Nowadays, the biggest everyday threat to most babies is a dirty diaper. However, if we missed that crucial window around three or four months of ages to gracefully allow our infants to learn independent sleep, we likely can expect some crying during this process. And we need to break our own habitual response to the crying at bedtime. The way to do this is to have a plan and follow through with it.

Of all the techniques in this book, this is the easiest to describe and the hardest to perform. In its purest form, you place your child in his crib after bedtime, close the door, and ignore his crying until he falls asleep. Many parents can't manage this, so I'll describe some variations that may help.

TO CHECK OR NOT TO CHECK: THAT IS THE QUESTION

In 1985, Dr. Richard Ferber published a little book called *Solve Your Child's Sleep Problems*, based on his experience at the Pediatric Sleep Program at Children's Hospital Boston. Remember sleep onset associations from earlier in the book? That is his theory, which has been borne out by scientific experimentation. Interestingly, his ideas about sleep evolved after wondering why his own children needed a parent to be present with them in order to go back to sleep. Ferber is such a big deal that his name has become a verb, "Ferberize"—a term he dislikes, as it oversimplifies his considerable body of work.

"Ferberizing" your child is a style of sleep training described in his book; technically, it's called graduated extinction. Just as in traditional CIO/extinction sleep training, you place your child in her crib and say good night. However, in the modified version, you go in and check on your child at set intervals. *Here's the critical part:*

a check is a short and simple visit to the room. You shouldn't pick your daughter up or soothe her to sleep. You go in and repeat your final bedtime cue, such as, "I love you. It's time to go to sleep. Good night," and leave the room. It's generally not a good idea to pick up your child, as she may immediately fall asleep—and then you have set the precedent that prolonged crying means you will "rescue" her.

In theory, checking on your child reassures her that everything is all right and also makes you feel better. In practice, it doesn't always work that way. With my son, checking backfired. He would calm down temporarily when we went in, but his crying when we left the room would redouble. Here's a dirty little secret about checking: it's for the parents. While checks can assuage parental guilt, they don't necessarily help the child fall asleep more quickly. Some evidence indicates that checks may even prolong the length of the CIO process.

Let me be clear: I'm not saying don't use checks. If using checks helps you stick with sleep training, I'm all for it. However, I *am* saying that they aren't necessary, and you need to decide if they help your child sleep more quickly or not. If you do decide to check on your child, here's how to do it.

1. **On the first night of CIO, try checking on your child at five minutes in.** Gauge her response *when you leave the room.* Does checking on her seem to have calmed her down, or does it seem to have revved her up? Do *you* need the checks for your peace of mind?
2. **If it seems helpful, continue checking at set intervals.** I like to keep the schedule simple because—let's be real—you're pretty tired.

   Night 1: every 5 minutes
   Night 2: every 10 minutes
   Night 3: every 15 minutes

3. **Go in if your child is screaming.** On the other hand, if she seems to be calming down, stay out of the room.

BEDTIME "FADING" TO MINIMIZE CRYING

Aggressively moving your child's bedtime later (a technique with the clunky name "faded bedtime with response cost") is another CIO-based method that involves progressively delaying bedtime to harness your child's natural sleep drive. This works well for parents who can't imagine allowing their child to cry for more than fifteen minutes but are interested in using the magic of CIO to rapidly improve sleep. This can work in a few days but does require a fair amount of parental energy and investment. Note that your child may be up pretty late for the first few nights. Here's how to do it:

- Place your child in his crib drowsy but awake and leave the room. For the sake of this example, let's assume this is at 8:00 p.m.
- After fifteen minutes of his crying, pick him up and calm him down.
- Keep him awake until 9:00 p.m. This can be pretty tricky.
- Put him down again and repeat your bedtime verbal cue at 9:00 p.m.
- If he continues to cry and does not fall asleep within fifteen minutes, get him out of bed and soothe him.
- Keep him awake until 10:00 p.m. and try again.
- Eventually, he will fall asleep within fifteen minutes of putting him down.
- Maintain his current wake time in the morning, and don't let him get extra sleep during his naps.
- Repeat the process on night two and subsequent nights until he is falling asleep within fifteen minutes at his bedtime.

There are a few reasons I am not fond of this method. The first reason is that it is difficult to keep your child awake while soothing him, especially as the night progresses. The other is that this is a bit complicated. Complexity is the enemy of success for tired parents. However, if the prospect of hearing your child cry for more than fifteen minutes is unbearable *and* if you can manage to keep your child awake, this is a helpful option. I remember one mom who was adamantly against allowing her child crying for prolonged periods, but also thought that "camping out" (described later) would not work. After some discussion, we settled on this method. She called me a few days later and told me that it had been hard for a few days—her child was tired and cranky—but eventually it had worked like a charm.

QUESTIONS AND ANSWERS ABOUT CIO

Q. What if my child vomits while crying?
A. Sounds gross, right? Unfortunately, some kids vomit when they have been crying. Although it sounds cruel, the best thing to do is to go in, clean your child up, replace any sheets and pajamas that you need to, tell your child you love him, and leave the room. If you are consistent about this, your child will stop vomiting. Remember, if you respond to this behavior, you run the risk of creating a habit of his vomiting every time your child is unhappy. You don't want this habit. (If your child is prone to vomiting, check with your pediatrician to make sure you aren't missing a condition like acid reflux, which could be contributing to his sleep problems.)

Q. How about if he poops?
A. Ah, the dreaded sleep deuce. I would change his diaper if he is awake but let it ride if he has fallen asleep.

Q. What if my partner can't handle the crying?

A. The best thing to do is to send your partner out of town for a few days. If this is not possible, suggest an evening engagement with friends for a few nights, or a set of earplugs and a good book.

Q. Night two is worse. What am I doing wrong?

A. You are in the extinction burst. This means that you are on the cusp of improvement. Keep doing what you're doing.

Q. My child has a history of trauma. Should I use CIO?

A. Generally, no. Kids with a history of trauma, recently adopted children, or children with attachment issues will be better served by using a different method.

Q. What if I'm worried that my child hurt himself?

A. Then you have to go into the room and check on him. Likewise, if your child jumps out of his crib, CIO may not be the best fit.

Q. What if my child threw his pacifier or teddy bear out of the crib?

A. In this scenario, I would not go in. This is simply a delaying tactic.

Q. What do I do if my child wakes up at night?

A. As discussed in Chapter 7, if your child wakes up within a few hours of bedtime, I suggest you repeat your bedtime plan of allowing him to cry, along with checking if you find that helpful. Later in the night, it is up to you if you want to repeat your bedtime plan or just rapidly soothe your child back to sleep so you can survive the next day.

Camping Out
Time to better sleep: Slow
Stress level: Medium
Best age range: Six months and up (instructions here are for kids in a crib; later I will show you how to use this for older children who are sleeping in a bed)

Maybe traditional CIO is not right for you. That is *totally* understandable. For young children, there's another technique that works well for many families. It goes under the cumbersome name "graduated extinction with parental presence," but I prefer the term "camping out," which was coined by Harriet Hiscock, a sleep psychologist in Australia (and the lead author on the best long-term study of sleep-training safety, which I referred to in Chapter 7). In this age group, I don't think that there is such a thing as a "no-cry" solution, but this may be much more palatable, as your child will not be alone.

Image courtesy of Ruth Fidino.

With this method, you "camp out" in your child's room until she falls asleep, and you continue to do this every night for several weeks. The difference is that every few days, you gradually scale back your involvement at bedtime.

After you have optimized your Bedtime Funnel and finished

all the hard work of Part Two, you are ready to start. Let's say that you normally rock your child to sleep. With camping out, you will start in contact with your child but work on slowly phasing out your involvement at sleep onset.

- During the first three nights, you will stay close to her and rub her back or belly to help her fall asleep. You continue this for three nights, until your child is falling asleep fairly easily. (In this example, I'll assume you do each step for three days, but you'll need to see how your child responds; it may go faster for some children, more slowly for others.)
- On the fourth night, you set a chair near her bed but you will not touch her. If your child cries, stands up, or demands more attention, you should not get into a discussion with her; you simply remain seated and repeat your final bedtime cue: "I love you. It's time to go to sleep. Good night." It's actually better to avoid eye contact, and perhaps look at an ebook reader or your smartphone. Although you are present, the goal of this method is still removal of your involvement in sleep onset. This means that you need to provide only minimal attention. You continue saying this when your child demands attention until she falls asleep.
- After you've done this for three more nights, next you will move your chair to a spot halfway between your child's bed and the door. Again, if she struggles or seems upset, repeat your final bedtime cue but don't pick her up or offer more attention.
- After she has mastered this step, the next steps are to first place a chair near or in the doorway for a few nights, and then outside the door, preferably out of sight. Again, make each transition once your child has successfully fallen asleep with minimum fuss for at least one night.

Although you are present, the goal of this method is still removal of your involvement for sleep onset. This means that you will need to provide minimal attention to your child. You should not get in a discussion with your child, but simply sit with her and repeat your final bedtime cue: "I love you. It's time to go to sleep. Good night." The interaction you provide should be basic and boring. (Remember, attention from you is the reward that powers the habit loop!)

Every few days, when your child has begun to fall asleep fairly easily, you can move a step further out. Each step should take about two to five days. After one night of sleep onset within fifteen minutes of lights-out, you can move to the next step. Here's a sample schedule based on making changes every three days.

- Days 1–3: You stand by his crib and rub his back.
- Days 4–6: You sit by your child's bedside but do not touch him.
- Days 7–9: You move your chair to midway between your child's bedside and the door.
- Days 10–12: You sit in your chair by the door to the room.
- Days 13–15: You sit outside the door but where your child can still see you.
- Days 16–18: You sit out of sight but provide verbal reassurance, either by sitting just outside the room or by using a two-way monitor.

The hardest steps are usually the second (sitting nearby but not touching) and the last one (moving outside your child's line of sight). These are when your willpower will be tested. Stay consistent, repeat your cue, and remember that you are doing this for the benefit of your whole family.

Raise your hand if you notice the downside of camping out relative to traditional CIO: this takes a long time. As I mentioned in

Chapter 7, you need to decide in advance if you will repeat your bedtime routine when your child wakes up, or just comfort the child as you had been doing previously. Many families choose the second route, as getting a child back to sleep with this method can take a long time.

You are not guaranteed that your child will just quietly go along with this. He may stand at the crib rail and cry. You will probably feel like a heel. Some families try this and then switch to regular CIO after seeing their child cry just as much, without the upside of quick results. That is OK.

QUESTIONS AND ANSWERS

Q. Wait, night two is worse than the first night. What gives?
A. You can have an extinction burst with this method as well. You need to stay consistent.

Q. What if he stands up?
A. Just stay in position and repeat your bedtime cue. Do not lay him back down, replace thrown binkies or teddy bears, or otherwise interact. This does get easier, but improvement will be slow and may take up to a week.

Techniques for the Bed Sleeper (Age Three and Up)

If you have a child who has graduated from a crib to a bed but resists falling asleep and staying asleep, I can guarantee two things. First, you are fed up and tired. This has likely been going on for years. Second, the conventional sleep-training techniques that you've heard of (like CIO) won't work. The child is too stubborn and strong for this to be practical—and most kids won't just stay in bed and cry. Don't despair! I have good news for you. There are several effective techniques for this age, including a particularly powerful kind of positive reinforcement: rewards. In this context, rewards don't always mean actual prizes. Sometimes, it is just positive, loving attention from you. Changing your child's sleep habits can even be fun. Approach this in the spirit of play. If you come from a place of dread or anger, your child will know it.

I've targeted this section toward children three and up because most will be sleeping in a bed. If your child has not yet graduated from a crib, you can still use these techniques. Likewise, you can try these techniques in a mature two-and-a-half-year-old if she is sleeping in a bed. That is probably the youngest age where a child can understand the relationship between her behavior and rewards. Finally, if you have not yet transitioned your child from a crib to a bed, I might do that first and let your child get used to the new situation before working on independent sleep. For more on taking that step, refer to Chapter 3.

Rehearsal

Confession time: I was a theater nerd in high school and college, acting, directing, and stage-managing. With any production, you spend a lot of time practicing all aspects of the show before opening night. Although at times it was grueling and frustrating, I loved it. My high school theater program had a tradition called "Toga Night." Two nights before opening night, we would run the play, but instead of our normal costumes, we would wear bedsheets safety-pinned in a rough approximation of a Roman robe. Cream pies to the face, dirty jokes, and rubber chickens substituted for key props were the norm. This goofy night took the edge off of everyone's nerves and reminded everyone to have fun.

I'm telling you this not because I'm suggesting you should throw a cream pie in your child's face when he comes out of his room at night for the tenth time (although that would be hilarious). My point is that practicing bedtime during the day can help both parents and children who are terrified about making changes to their sleep routine. Older children love make-believe, and pretending that you are doing bedtime in the middle of the day can be silly fun for everyone. You can even start having your child put you to bed in her room first.

No matter what technique you select, rehearsing it with your child will help it go more smoothly. If your child is really anxious (or if you are), you can practice a few times before you start making changes at bedtime. There are a few principles for successful rehearsal:

- **Make it fun.** Act goofy. Pretend to be the child and have your child be the parent first. Get into your pajamas if you have time. Have your child practice putting her teddy bear to bed. If you don't make it fun, your child will be as unexcited about it as she is about her real bedtime.

- **Do it at least a few times per week.** I know this can be difficult for working parents. The more you practice, the better it will go, but if you can only rehearse on the weekends, that is fine.

- **Rehearse at least a few hours before bedtime.** You don't want to do this right before actual bedtime—that's often already a fraught time. Rather, do it in the morning before school, or in the afternoon.

- **Do a mini version of bedtime and your sleep-training technique.** You don't actually have to brush teeth and read a story (although you can), but go through all the steps of bedtime and the technique you choose below.

- **Reward a good rehearsal.** If you are using a reward system (discussed later in this chapter), provide the same reward for your child for success in a rehearsal as you do for success in the actual bedtime technique. Also, *round up*—if your child comes close to doing what you are asking, give the reward. Finally, remember that the best reward is extravagant praise from you.

Camping Out for Big Kids
Time to better sleep: Slow
Stress level: Medium
Best age range: Any age

Camping out can also work for older children who sleep in beds. The general principle is the same, but the execution is slightly different. Just as previously described, you will stay in your child's room until he falls asleep. Over the course of a week or two, you will gradually increase your distance from your child's bed. You should not engage in conversation; simply repeat your bedtime mantra: "I love you. It's time to go to sleep. Good night." Older kids may need more of an explanation for why you are sitting there ignoring them. Otherwise, the five-year-old is going to give you a look that says, "What the hell are you doing?" Be open about the fact that you know he is a big kid but needs a little help falling asleep. It's fine to say that you have to do a bit of work while you are waiting for him to fall asleep but that if he interrupts you, you'll have to leave the room. This is one of the few situations where it would be OK for you to sit with your phone while ignoring your child. Make sure you have the brightness turned down, and recognize that this initially may be distracting to your child.

If you say you're going to leave the room if he gets out of his bed, you need to follow through. My mentor Dr. Judy Owens gives parents this procedure: If your child will not stay in his bed, leave the room and close the door for one minute. When you open the door, the expectation is that he is back in his bed. If he is not, close the door for two minutes. Repeat as necessary, adding a minute each time, until your child is in bed when you reopen the door. As you can imagine, this can get ugly on the first few nights you try it. There can be some crying, or even an extinction burst, as this is an extinction-based method (you are ignoring behaviors you don't like). I don't really recommend this for children who are very anxious or who struggle with attachment, as it can be very traumatic. The progressive breaks method, described next, may be a better fit.

Progressive Breaks

Time to better sleep: Medium to slow, depending on your child

Stress level: Low

Best age range: Three years and up

Progressive breaks slowly peel back your involvement at bedtime. They work really well for anxious children (and anxious parents). The idea is that you are expecting your child to deal with your absence for short periods of time, which gradually increase. When you return, you praise your child like she just won the Nobel Prize. Tell her, "Look at you in your bed like a big girl! You look so comfortable and cozy! I am so proud of you for staying put and relaxing, just like we talked about. I knew you could do it!" The praise should be over the top, and if you don't feel a bit embarrassed at how enthusiastic you're being, lay it on thicker. Hugs and kisses help as well, though avoid crawling into your child's bed if you can. If your child is a bit older—think nine or ten—she may find this corny; some verbal praise and perhaps a high five may be a better fit. Remember, praise and attention from you is the most reinforcing consequence you have to offer your child.

For both of these techniques, you need to have an idea of how long it takes your child to fall asleep after you turn out the lights. If your child currently needs you to be with her in order for her to fall asleep, I suspect you have a pretty good idea. Let's say that you turn off the lights at 8:00 p.m. and she falls asleep at 8:20 p.m. During that twenty-minute period, you will be leaving the room to "take a break" for a brief interval halfway through, then returning. If your child is taking a long time to fall asleep (more than thirty minutes), consider a later bedtime, as described in "A Reminder on Timing" earlier in the chapter. When you start, these breaks should be very short—about a minute long. They can be shorter if your child absolutely cannot stay in bed without you present for that length of time; parents of anxious little ones may have to start with fifteen- or thirty-second breaks.

The principle behind these methods is that you are slowly increasing the capacity of your child to be alone at night. The goal is for your child to fall asleep during one of the breaks. *If she does, still follow through on your promise to return to the room.* It is critical that you keep your word. If she is asleep, however, don't wake her up.

I'm going to describe two variations of progressive breaks. Most families will do better with the first version, where you take a single break that lengthens with time, although children who are very anxious or have developmental delay may do better with the second, which consists of multiple small breaks.

TAKING A BREAK

This is one of my favorite methods in this book because (a) it works really well and (b) it doesn't feel like sleep training, because it is so gentle. You will select a time to take a break that is midway between lights-out and falling asleep. Below, I'm going to use our example of 8:00 p.m. lights-out with 8:20 p.m. sleep onset. Here's how to do it:

- Rehearse this once or twice during the day so your child knows what to expect.

- Go through your bedtime routine—potentially at a later time, as noted in "A Reminder on Timing."
- At 8:10 p.m., tell your child that you are taking a break. Leave the room and promise to come back quickly. You *don't* have to tell your child how long the break will be, as you don't want to encourage clock watching.
- Return in one minute and praise the child extravagantly, knowing that your Oscar nomination will be in the mail. "Look what a big boy you are! You stayed in bed and are so cozy! Great job!" Hugs and kisses are OK.
- Stay until your child falls asleep.
- The next night, do the same thing, except leave for two minutes.

Usually this does not require further rewards. Older kids may benefit from them, however, so you can leave a reward token, as described in the "Reward Systems" section later in this chapter.

THE EXCUSE ME DRILL

The Excuse Me Drill was developed by Dr. Brett Kuhn to address the sleep challenges of children with Angelman syndrome, a rare disorder associated with developmental delay and severe sleep difficulties. This involves multiple short breaks during bedtime and works well for children who resist even brief absences. However, it requires a high level of energy from you. Just as I did in the last example, we will use our planned timing of 8:00 p.m. lights-out with 8:20 p.m. sleep onset. As before, rehearse this once or twice so your child knows what to expect. Here's how to do it:

- Go through your bedtime routine (potentially at a later time, as noted in "A Reminder on Timing").
- A little bit after lights-out, tell your child that you need to

step out for a moment to do something. (This is called the Excuse Me Drill because you say something along the lines of, "Excuse me for a minute—I need to check the soufflé/basketball scores/price of Bitcoin." (During the evening keep these excuses mundane, but during rehearsal it is fun to make them silly.) Note that you will feel ridiculous.

- Stay out for a very short period of time. Return and praise the child extravagantly. As before, lay it on thick.
- A little bit later, step out again for a very brief interval.

On night one, you will do this multiple times (think twenty to thirty repetitions of stepping out, pausing for less than a minute, then returning). Every time you come back in, provide the affection and attention that reinforces the bravery of your child in being apart from you. Doing this frequently is called a "thick" reinforcement schedule. After about thirty minutes of this, it's OK to stay with your child until he falls asleep.

On night two, you will gradually increase the amount of time you spend out of the room. Each night the breaks will be longer and longer until your child starts falling asleep without you.

Reward Systems

For parents of older children (age three and up) who struggle with difficult bedtimes (tantrums, yelling, stomping, and throwing things—not to mention your child's behavior), using a reward system can be just the ticket for success. A reward system requires some thought and care to put into place, so other techniques may be easier to implement. However, reward systems can be really effective if you have tried the other methods but still face resistance.

Now, let me get a few misconceptions out of the way. First, rewards are not bribes. Bribes are payments for future behavior you hope to see—say, slipping your child a twenty so he will never hit his younger brother again. As you can imagine, they don't work. Rewards are won by good behavior—like allowing your child an extra five minutes of screen time if he can avoid fighting with his brother when brushing his teeth in the morning. Second, rewards are in addition to the lavish praise I described above; they are not a substitute for it. Think of rewards as a cue for you to offer praise.

For most children, a simple reward system (such as the Bedtime Pass or the Sleep Fairy, both of which are discussed later) will work pretty well. This means that your child will receive a token for behavior that you have agreed upon previously. (A sticker or a poker chip in a jar work well for younger kids; for older children, a check mark or star on a chart are just as effective. For kids who are past the first few grades in elementary school, you may need to put in place a more complex economy.)

Using rewards can be tricky. If you want to use them, here are the critical points you need to remember for success:

- **Decide what behavior you are rewarding and be clear about it.** For the simple systems, the goal is for your child to stay in her room by herself. Tell her very clearly what you would like her to do, and practice it during your rehearsals. This is just like our bedtime cue. A good cue is "I want you to go upstairs and brush your teeth." A bad cue would be something like "Go get ready for bed."

- **Rehearsals earn rewards.** If you are using rehearsals, give the same rewards that you would at bedtime.

- **Reward things your child can control.** Your child cannot control when she falls asleep. Neither can you or I—we can just set conditions for sleep and hope it comes. That's why the steps in Part Two of this book are so important. That's also why bedtime fading (moving bedtime to a time when your child falls asleep within thirty minutes) is critical. You can reward your child for staying in bed when you leave the room, or for getting ready for bed without a fight, but not for falling asleep at an exact time.

- **When giving rewards, round up.** Parents may worry that their child will game the system. That is not the right way to think about rewards. *The goal is for your child to succeed.* You want your child to get the rewards. If you have agreed that you want your child to brush his teeth and get his pajamas on in five minutes, and he gets it done in six, give him the reward. Don't be too strict.

- **Have a plan for when the rewards will end.** You don't want to be rewarding your child for brushing his teeth when he is seventeen. Also, rewards tend to lose their value over time. Usually you want to work toward a cumulative goal in addition to a nightly goal. Decide on a target for a larger reward (for example, if your child stays in her bed at night for a certain number of days, you'll take her for dinner at a favorite restaurant, or she can have a playdate with a friend at a favorite playground, a sleepover with a best friend, or a desired toy). Typically, your child should be able to attain this in a month. One good way to do this is to put a poker chip next to your child's bed as a token. Each night that she accomplishes the goal you've agreed on, she can put this chip in a jar. When the jar gets filled to a certain level, you then give her the larger reward and tell her that she is now a big girl and doesn't need this system anymore.

- **Don't take anything away.** If you take something away and then offer your child the chance to earn it back, that is a punishment, not a reward. Taking away Legos or screen time will only backfire.

WHAT ARE GOOD REWARDS?

Rewards need to be specific to your child. You probably have a better idea of what she would find motivating than I would. If your child gets to help pick them out, even better. These do not need to cost much (or any) money. As I've noted before, special time and attention from you is the best reward. You also need to make sure that you can deliver the reward when asked (within reason). I encourage you to make a list and post it prominently in your home, either on your refrigerator or where your child sleeps.

Here are some ideas for daily rewards:

- Five minutes of screen time
- Picking a favorite dinner for the family
- Picking a favorite TV show
- Picking a board game for the family to play
- A trip to the playground of his choice
- Breakfast in bed on the weekend
- Small stickers or toys (the sort of thing you might find at the dollar store)

Consider these larger rewards (for a cumulative goal of, say, seven good nights in a row or getting a smaller reward fourteen times):

- A special outing with a parent (such as going ice skating or to the nail salon)
- A sleepover with a friend or cousin
- A special dinner out with your family
- A trip to visit a special relative such as grandparents
- A strongly desired toy or item

The Sleep Fairy
Time to better sleep: A week
Stress level: Low
Best age range: Three to five years
Best for: Children who just need a little incentive to stay in their room at night

Does your child believe in the Tooth Fairy? Is he not creeped out by the idea of a magical being who sneaks into his room at night and buys a piece of his body that he has placed under his pillow? (I know, I feel weird about it, too. I also am embarrassed to admit how much money "the Tooth Fairy" pays for my kids' teeth.) Then talking up the Sleep Fairy may be useful for you if you just want your child to "get over the hump" and stay in his room at night.

- Explain to your child that the Sleep Fairy is coming to visit him for a few weeks. You can say that the Sleep Fairy is friends with the Tooth Fairy and that she comes around and checks on little kids who are trying to fall asleep.
- After your child falls asleep at night, place a small reward (a toy or modest amount of money) under your child's pillow.
- After two weeks, tell your child that he has done a great job and that the Sleep Fairy has to help other kids that need her more, but that she will check on him a few more times. Provide a few more rewards (every two or three days, on an inconsistent schedule).

Once you stop, leave a nice note from the Sleep Fairy congratulating your child on his success!

The Bedtime Pass

Time to better sleep: A week or two, depending on your child

Stress level: Low

Best age range: Three to eight years

Best for: Children who come out of their room a lot at bedtime or during the night

The Bedtime Pass is a favorite of mine. It's a great, simple reward system if you are struggling with frequent curtains calls at bedtime, or even if you have a child who gets up occasionally at night. Each night your child gets a pass that allows her to come out of her room and make one request—such as for an extra hug, a drink of water, or a story. If she doesn't use the pass that night, you give her a small reward the next day.

Just as with all reward systems, you want to set this system up for your child to succeed. If your child usually comes out of her room four times at night, she will fail if you only use one pass, so you can start with two or three, then gradually reduce the number of passes she can use each night.

Here's how you use the Bedtime Pass.

1. **Make a nice card with your child that says "Bedtime Pass" and decorate it.** Glitter is good; lamination, even better. If you think you need more, make two or three.
2. **Your child keeps the pass in her room and can redeem it once for a simple request from Mom or Dad (one more story, a glass of water, a back rub, etc.).** The request should be brief and easy for you to do (it should *not* be lying down with your child for thirty minutes).
3. **After redeeming it, she turns in the pass.** If she comes out again, you return her silently to her room with minimal interaction.

4. **If she does not use the pass, she can redeem it the next day for a small reward.** In addition to the reward, make sure you give your child a lot of praise as well.

5. **If you are using more than one pass, remove one every week (or even sooner if things are going well).** Exchange it by letting your child "buy" one of her rewards, or even a slightly larger reward.

6. **Make giving up the last pass a special occasion.** For example, giving up the last pass can earn your child a larger cumulative reward.

You can adapt a similar system if your child gets up too early in the morning, by saying that your child can use her pass during the times you expect her to stay in her room. So if she wakes up at 5:30 a.m., she has to use a pass if she wants to get you before 6:00 a.m.

Note also that your child is still allowed to leave her room to go to the bathroom or get a drink of water—by herself. We want to encourage independent behavior at night.

More Elaborate Reward Systems

Time to better sleep: A few weeks
Stress level: Medium
Best age range: Six to twelve years
Best for: Children who act out around bedtime

Rewards can work well for children with more complex behavioral needs as well, both those with developmental delay and older children with more established patterns of difficulty around sleep. With rewards, you can work in a very granular way on each step of your child's bedtime.

Dr. Alan Kazdin is the director of the Yale Parenting Center. He has written a number of parenting books, my favorite being *The*

Kazdin Method for Parenting the Defiant Child. Don't be put off by the title—whose child isn't defiant sometimes?

Dr. Kazdin recommends using a more detailed reward system that tracks the goals you are working on. He recommends that working on one or two goals at a time is the best method, and I agree. He recommends rehearsal as well, including dispensing rewards for it. This is a good fit for a child who really acts out at bedtime. (If you are dealing with simple curtain calls, you might want to try the Bedtime Pass instead.)

For this to succeed, you need to be very clear about what your goals are, decide what steps are needed to get your child there, and reward the behavior you are working toward. Let's take the example of a six-year-old boy named Henry who raises hell every time his parents tell him to go upstairs to bed.

1. Move lights-out to the time that Henry typically falls asleep.
2. Announce to Henry that we are now going to be playing a game to win prizes for being good at bedtime. He can win points at bedtime and during the day as well.
3. Identify what he needs to do to succeed. In this case, his parents want him to go to his room, put his pajamas on, and get into bed without fighting.
4. Immediately go into rehearsal of his bedtime so that he can earn points and potentially a reward (described in more detail later). You don't have to do rehearsals every day, but fit in as many as you can.
5. At bedtime, provide a clear, unequivocal cue. Say, "Henry, it's time to get ready for bed now." (Use this in your rehearsal.)
6. If he earns his points, reward him and make a big deal about it with extravagant praise. Don't add on what Dr. Kazdin calls a caboose, or negative statement (for example: "Great job! Why can't you do this every night?").

7. If he doesn't meet his goals, announce calmly that he will not get points but will have another opportunity tomorrow.

How to Set Up the Points

1. Decide whether you are going to use concrete tokens (such as poker chips) or just keep score on a sheet.

2. Two points per task is a good number, because you can reward with half credit. Say, if you want him to get his pajamas on and get into bed on his own, if he puts his pajamas on but then comes out of the room, you can award partial credit.

3. Round up when rewarding points. If he does most of what you want, award full credit. Remember, you want him to succeed.

4. Don't remove points for misbehavior unrelated to the task you are working on (such as throwing food at dinner, prior to the beginning of the bedtime sequence). You can remove points if, say, he goes in his room, gets into his pajamas, then leaves the room and starts a fire in the bathtub.

5. He needs to be able to buy a reward the first time he succeeds. In this example, some rewards should cost one or two points.

You can also track progress toward a big reward. This has the added benefit of providing a way to finish with the reward system. When Henry reaches his goal, celebrate his success and explain that he doesn't need the points for bedtime anymore. Many parents find these systems so useful that they move on to using point/reward systems for other challenges (in my house, it's getting the kids to practice piano).

You can add in the Bedtime Pass as well. If your child doesn't use it, he can redeem it for two more points. This is useful if you are working on having your child get ready for bed without incident but also want to incentivize staying in his room at night.

For Single Parents

Implementing any sleep-training plan can be challenging for couples but even harder for single parents. It's not impossible, however, and the potential rewards are even greater since self-care is particularly important if you are on call twenty-four hours a day without anyone to back you up. I have a few suggestions if you feel alone in this process:

1. **Ask for help.** It is reasonable to ask grandparents or friends to help you out. I know you don't want to impose, but trust me—your closest friends and family likely already know that you are struggling and have been waiting for you to ask for help. Don't be afraid to ask someone to take your child for an afternoon, or even a night. Some people may even be willing to come over to your house for a night or two.
2. **Pick a time that is good for you to start.** Maybe you don't have the bandwidth right now. Just stick with a good bedtime and wait for, say, summer vacation or a slow period at work.
3. **Give yourself a break.** Your child's sleep will improve with time if you are consistent. Don't feel like everything needs to be perfect. Sometimes your kid's socks will be all over her bedroom, or you will want to eat out for dinner instead of cooking. That's OK. Your child knows you are doing your best.

For Children with Medical or Special Needs

Every child has different challenges. Many of the children I care for in the Sleep Center have medical issues or developmental delay. If your child has special needs, do not give up on the possibility of good sleep! I'm a firm believer that every child and every parent deserve satisfying rest.

If your child has medical issues, it's critical to make sure that they are under control. For example, children with eczema who are itching all night will not be able to sleep well. (See Chapter 2 for some common underlying issues of sleep difficulties.) If your child needs medical equipment during the night (say, feeding via tube or receiving supplemental oxygen), it can be a little bit tricky. Incorporate this technology into your child's bedtime routine—for many children, taking medication or attaching their feeding tube is routine behavior at night. It's also critical not to pity your child. Your goals for this child may be different than for your other children, but you still should set expectations for behavior and reward them, even if you have to allow for their particular needs.

Children with autism especially struggle with sleep. Two books I highly recommend if your child is on the autism spectrum are *Solving Sleep Problems in Children with Autism Spectrum Disorders: A Guide for Frazzled Families* by Beth Malow and Terry Katz, and *Sleep Better! A Guide to Improving Sleep for Kids with Special Needs* by V. Mark Durand. Dr. Malow and Dr. Durand have children with autism and know the subject intimately, both professionally and personally. If you continue to struggle, working with a child psychiatrist, psychologist, or sleep doctor can be very helpful.

ACTION ITEMS

1. Select a technique from this chapter and get started! It is important that you execute a strategy consistently for a week or two. Don't be paralyzed by choice, however. It is better to get started than to agonize over this.

2. Decide in advance how you will deal with the middle-of-the-night awakenings. Will you apply your bedtime consequence plan? Or will you soothe your child back to sleep?

3. Do not be discouraged by an extinction burst. It will likely get worse before it gets better—but if you can work through this period, you'll be rewarded with better sleep for your whole family. Remind yourself why you are doing this: look back at the reasons you wrote down for why you want to improve your child's sleep.

CHAPTER 9

STAYING IN THE (HABIT) LOOP

IF YOU'VE MADE it this far, congratulations! I know that you have worked hard to improve sleep for your whole family. There are two possible outcomes if you have followed the program described in this book.

The first, most likely result is that your child is sleeping much better at night. I hope you are as well. Enjoy the fruits of your labors and the satisfaction of feeling like a normal human being again. If this is the case, there are a few steps to make sure that your child continues to sleep well—and to ensure that you don't panic at the first sign of trouble.

The second possible result is that things are still not going according to plan. I'm going to review some persistent challenges, including bedtime issues, nighttime awakenings, and how to address the dreaded early morning wake-up calls.

Locking in High-Quality Sleep: How to Maintain

If things have gone well, you are probably pretty nervous at this point. In the past, you may have experienced a night or two of blissful, uninterrupted sleep, only to have the old patterns reassert themselves for weeks or months. I promise you that because you have used the habit loop to shape your child's behavior, this time is different. There are a few things you need to do to lock in these habits and make them effortless. It's like learning to ride a bike. When you start, you have to think about every move, and one bad fall can shake your confidence. With time, the riding becomes automatic and you can enjoy your ride without struggling to stay upright.

Remember, habits take about a month to become established and automatic. This is the case for both you and your child. As we talked about back in Chapter 2, good sleep habits are actually two sets of interlocking habits—yours and your child's. So if you've finally achieved good sleep, celebrate your hard work, but don't relax just yet.

First, you need to be consistent for a month. I don't mean a month from when you started—I mean a month from when your child's sleep improved. During this time, I recommend avoiding trips, visits from family, or any other major disruptions to your routine if at all possible. Getting a babysitter so that you can go out for an evening is OK if you have confidence that it will not disrupt your child's routine. (Generally, most kids behave better for their babysitters than for their parents—parental attention is a much more desirable consequence than attention from a babysitter. However, I remember one babysitter who did not put my son to bed because he didn't want to go. Needless to say, my wife and I were not excited to have to do bedtime after a nice evening out. This prompted me to half-jokingly coin the Second Canapari Rule for future sitters— if the kids are awake when I get home, you don't get paid.) If you have to go to your brother's wedding, consider leaving your child with caregivers who will respect your routines, or bring your child with you but reproduce your cues and consequences as consistently as possible. If you are staying in a hotel, this means keeping the same approximate bedtime and bedtime routine, but this can be difficult if you are sharing a room after getting your child to sleep independently. This is an imperfect solution and may result in a temporary setback; I'll talk later about how to deal with this.

After the first consistent month of high-quality sleep, you can relax a bit, but not entirely. After this, it's OK to allow variation on one or two nights per week, such as going out to dinner at another family's house or an outing to the movies. Recognize that this may result in a little sleep disruption, but stay confident in the system that you have put in place.

The final thing to remember is not to panic if you have a bad night or two. This happens to everyone, and actually can be expected at certain times.

When to Expect Trouble, and How to Troubleshoot

Sometimes I get panicked calls from parents I last saw six months earlier. "She was sleeping great," they say breathlessly, "but now she is waking up again!" As a parent, I have often experienced the feeling of panic that occurs when a seemingly solved problem comes back. (Like the time we were deep in the woods hiking and my then four-year-old was swarmed by mosquitoes and pooped his pants. "Meet me at the trailhead!" read the panicked text I sent to my wife. "Bring wipes, a trash bag, and a clean pair of pants.") You are not going to be psyched. But you need to calm down and stop panicking. And I'm not just telling you this for your mental health. Remember, *any* attention—positive or negative—you give to behavior you don't like will just reinforce that behavior. If you freak out the first time your child comes into your room at night after a month of good sleep, you run the risk of kick-starting another habit loop.

There are certain circumstances that seem to be associated with episodes of difficult sleep. I'll discuss each of them and offer some suggestions.

Sleep Regression

Here's a secret—when your pediatrician says, "Your child is going through a phase," she means, "Your child is doing something inexplicable and annoying and I hope it will pass soon, because I'm not sure what to do about it." This is commonly used to refer to episodes of sleep disruption that seem to come out of nowhere in children who have been sleeping well—the dreaded sleep regression.

I don't love the term "sleep regression." This is a term that has gained a lot of currency in parenting circles and among sleep consultants—a sleep coach named Rob Lindeman did a little legwork and found that this phrase started becoming popular around 2008, according to Google search data—but it does not correspond to any real physiologic change in the sleep of children. What parents typically mean when they use this term is an unexpected or unexplained disruption in their child's sleep. Many parents experience one when their infants develop an understanding of object permanence around four to six months of age: the child has a normal biological awakening at night, starts to realize that Mom or Dad is not there, and starts crying.

As it turns out, sleep disruption is often associated with new developmental attainments. As Dr. Danny Lewin, a sleep psychologist at Children's National Health System, says of sleep regression, "Don't see it as a setback or a problem, see it as a sign. Something is going on developmentally that in most common cases is a positive, emerging change in their development." It's hard to know exactly how this works in preverbal children. I'm always fascinated by the relationship between milestones in preverbal children and sleep disruption. I often wonder if kids are so excited about these attainments that they want to practice when they wake up at night. Or perhaps they are tired or sore.

Common developmental attainments associated with sleep disruption include:

The concurrent evolution of crawling, the notion of object permanence, and stranger anxiety (6–9 months)

Learning to walk (12–15 months)

Potty training (2–4 years)

Understanding of narrative in TV shows and movies (6–8 years)—when kids can better understand cause and effect (for example, in stories with "good guys" and "bad guys"), it can be associated with more anxiety, which often flares up at night

Another thing you need to look at if your child starts having sleep disruption is the media your child is exposed to. My boys are three years apart in age, and the younger one is more interested in his big brother's cool shows and video games than in more age-appropriate material. This is how he ended up watching *Ghostbusters* at age six. It didn't really scare him, but, honestly, it is not appropriate for that age. Sometimes even age-appropriate media can include images that resonate negatively with your child and really scare him. I remember having problems sleeping after seeing some freaky swamp monsters on the TV cartoon *Super Friends*. This is nothing, however, compared with the nighttime anxiety I had after seeing the commercial for *The Day After*—a movie featuring a nuclear attack on the United States—at age ten. I frantically prayed every night for months that there would not be a nuclear war that night. If your older child is struggling, ask him if there is something he is afraid of.

Minor Illnesses

Illnesses are less predictable than developmental changes but can be equally disruptive. Most commonly, these take the form of infections—such as the common cold, ear infections, or stomach bugs. They can also be due to flares of underlying issues—worsening itching from eczema, coughing and wheezing in a child with asthma, or even plain old constipation. In the throes of your child's illness, do your best to maintain your schedule, but don't get upset if your child needs you during the night. Fortunately, the associated sleep disruptions tend to go away when the illness does, provided that you go back to your routine.

Vacations

Remember when vacations were times of rest and repose, when you and your partner would enjoy long, late meals with a few cocktails, sleep in the next day, and then relax on the beach? Me neither.

In case you haven't figured it out yet, vacations with young kids can be wonderful, but they are not restful. When you disrupt your normal routine, you start to appreciate the importance of structure to your child's behavior. You may be staying with other families who have different schedules and rules around bedtime. You are likely sharing a room with your child. You may be eating different foods, and you and your child may have more face time than usual, which can result in frayed nerves. And I can guarantee that you will not be sleeping in unless your spouse or another family member whisks your children away at the crack of dawn. (My younger son is our lark, always up early in the morning. I remember going to Disney World and taking him for a walk before dawn on several mornings so that my wife and older son could sleep in—until 6:30 a.m.).

Here is some information I've picked up in our adventures about maximizing sleep:

- **Respect the routine.** When we go on vacation, we try really hard to maintain our kids' sleep times. This was harder when they used to nap. Of course, we bend the rules for special occasions such as weddings, concerts, or movies. Also, some "sneaky sleep" may be unavoidable, as the kids will be pretty tuckered out.

- **Recognize that other families have different rules, and be flexible.** My kids always point out to me when other families we are with have different rules (usually if the kids have more iPad time than mine). This can be pretty challenging when some kids go to bed later or get up earlier than your kids. Make sure your kids know that their friends or cousins might have different rules, and that it's OK. Encourage your children to be flexible and recognize differences in other families. Adults can also help with this process. I always appreciate that my sister-in-law, who allows her kids more screen time than we do with ours, encourages her children to abide by our rules when we are together so that everyone can play.

- **Go to bed early.** We were vacationing with cousins, and all the kids got up earlier than normal. If you want to catch up on your sleep, your best chance is to go to bed earlier than normal.

- **Make the room dark.** Close the curtains if they are present. Don't hesitate to hang towels over the windows if you need to; that can help your kids sleep a bit longer in the morning. You can drape a towel or blanket over a Pack 'n Play for kids older than a year, bring KidCo PeaPod travel beds for toddlers, or try a DreamTent (available at www.mydreamtents.com) for older kids.

- **Masking sound is important.** We usually bring our sound machines, but you can also run a fan or use an app on your phone for white noise or nature sounds (I use the Naturespace app).

- **Get creative with the sleeping arrangements.** Several years ago, we were staying with several cousins at a vacation home. Our older son shared a "room" (actually a walk-in closet) with his six-year-old cousin. That way they did not have to get up with their younger siblings (and tired parents) the next day. Of course, this is not perfect; my niece got up at 5:15 a.m. on the first day and woke our son as well. Sharing rooms can be a bit tricky for children used to having their own room; older children should be instructed to let others sleep if they wake up early. They may also be a bit chatty at bedtime, but that is part of the fun. One of the challenges can be a need for bed sharing, especially if you just weaned your child out of this arrangement. I encourage you to put your child in a Pack 'n Play (of course adhering to safe sleep guidelines) or, for older children, on an air mattress. If you do end up needing to share a bed with your child, explain carefully that this is a "special sleepover" and that the rules are different than at home. You may get a little pushback when you get home, but stick to your cues and consequences and your routine should quickly return to normal.

- **Jet lag can be tricky.** Jet lag occurs when traveling across time zones east or west, when your body clock is out of phase from the clock time. You can prepare a bit by putting your kids to bed later for a few days before traveling west or getting them up a bit earlier before traveling east. The main consequence can be a really early bedtime and wake time when traveling west, or vice versa when traveling east. Children tend to adapt quickly if they have exposure to natural light. Avoid "sneaky sleep" if possible, and try to get to the "correct" (according to the clock) bedtime as soon as possible. For short trips, an alternative may be keeping your home time zone schedule.

- **Don't forget the teddy bear.** This one is pretty self-explanatory.

Don't forget it at home. Don't forget it in the rental car, or the airport, or the diner. Trust me—I've been burned before.

What to Do If You Are Still Having Trouble

Sometimes, in spite of your best efforts, you may have some lingering difficulties. If you have followed the techniques in this book but continue to struggle after a few weeks, I recommend continuing with your bedtime cue but perhaps pause using consequences until you can figure out what isn't working.

First, look again for medical issues that may be affecting your child's sleep by making an appointment with your pediatrician. In Chapter 2, I list common problems that can disrupt sleep at night. It may even be worth considering an overnight sleep test to looking for a disorder such as obstructive sleep apnea.

Other persistent issues can be addressed by paying close attention to bedtime and the habit cycle. Sometimes a small adjustment can have big results. Here are some of the most common interventions to try if your child is still having a hard time.

Problems with Falling Asleep

TRY A LATER BEDTIME

If your child is still struggling to fall asleep at night, it may be worth revisiting your child's bedtime—specifically, when you turn the lights out. Go back to your sleep diaries for the past two or three days and look at the time your child is actually falling asleep. Then move your child's lights-out time to the time he is actually falling asleep. Here's the key—keep his wake time constant. Once he is falling asleep within fifteen to twenty minutes, move his bedtime earlier by ten minutes every few nights until you get back to

8:30 p.m. or earlier. For more on this process, called "bedtime fading," see Chapter 8.

CHECK FOR HIDDEN CONSEQUENCES

Look carefully at any inadvertent consequences you or others at home are providing. Usually this appears as a lack of consistency. Here are a few questions you can ask yourself:

1. Are bedtime and nap time happening at the same time consistently?
2. Is the bedtime routine the same every night?
3. Are you responding consistently to your child in the way you planned?
4. Is everyone who cares for your child (you, your spouse, Grandma, the sitter) doing the same things at bedtime and during the night? Work to eliminate any inconsistencies you uncover.

CONSIDER GETTING RID OF THE NAP

If you are ready to throw this book into the trash at the thought of getting rid of your child's nap, I don't blame you. I remember the blissful hours when my boys would sleep in the afternoon and I could work, run on the treadmill, read a book, or even nap myself. My older son was a champion napper and could go from 3:00 to 5:00 p.m. and still fall asleep by 8:00 p.m. We even had one month where my boys were napping at the same time, until my older son gave it up.

Some children just won't fall asleep at a reasonable hour if they have an afternoon nap. A study published in 2015 looked at the relationship between napping and nighttime sleep. This was a meta-analysis, a kind of study that combines data from multiple other studies (twenty-six studies of children between birth and five years of age, with a total of over seven hundred children). The authors found that napping after age two was associated with falling asleep later, getting less sleep at night, and having a poorer quality of night sleep (read: more awakenings). Studies like this get lots of press, with headlines like "Report Suggests Napping After Age Two Could Spoil Sleep." The lead author of this study, Karen Thorpe, was much less alarmist, noting that the evidence around napping is limited.

So, what does this mean for you? If your child is older than age two (or preferably a bit older—say, closer to three), is not falling asleep until 9:00 or 10:00 p.m., and is still taking a significant nap (more than an hour), you may want to experiment with getting rid of the nap. Often this will make bedtime and the night go better—at the cost of a grumpier kid during the late afternoon. This is an occasion where you may need to pick your poison—a child who's cranky in the afternoon and goes to bed by 7:30 p.m., or a child who's energetic in the afternoon and falls asleep around 9:30 or 10:00 p.m.

Also, as we talked about in Chapter 6, make sure you are avoiding "sneaky sleep" in the car or stroller in the later afternoon. Unplanned naps can ruin the best-planned bedtimes.

One common complaint I hear from parents is that their child has a mandatory nap period in daycare or preschool. Older children (think three and up) who don't really need a nap may still sleep if they are expected to lie on a mat in a room of sleeping children with nothing to do. Parents complain that such children stay up late on school nights, but on weekends will refuse to nap and then go to sleep earlier. A study in Australia looked at the relationship between mandatory nap periods and nighttime sleep. The study, which involved 168 children between fifty and seventy-two months (about four to six years), found that mandatory one-hour nap periods were associated with a decrease of over thirty minutes of sleep per night.

In my practice, I've seen a more dramatic difference, with marked difficulty at bedtime for children who don't really need a nap but have to take one.

If you are concerned about the effect of your childcare center's policies on your child's sleep, I encourage you to sit down with the director and discuss them. If your child does not nap on weekends or vacations (or if you are trying to eliminate the nap to improve nighttime sleep), ask if the center can provide an alternative quiet activity such as reading or coloring. If the teachers give you a hard time or are inflexible about your child's needs, it may be worth looking for a new childcare situation.

Problems with Staying Asleep

If your child resists falling asleep and still wakes up frequently at night, I encourage you to follow the steps in the preceding "Problems with Falling Asleep" section. However, if your child has been falling asleep independently for a few weeks yet is still having troublesome nighttime awakenings, here are a few techniques that can work. Pick one that feels like a good fit for your parenting style and try it out for a week or two.

THE SILENT RETURN

If you really want your child to stay in his room at night, you can try a technique that Dr. Marc Weissbluth calls the "silent return." The idea is that you will wordlessly escort your child back to his room *every* time he gets up. The silence is essential—remember that *any* attention from you, be it yelling, hugging, crying, or jumping up and down on a pogo stick—is a reinforcing consequence and is likely to perpetuate the awakenings. Your child is looking for contact from you, so you need to minimize it. You can use your final bedtime cue (for example, "I love you. It's time to go to sleep. Good night").

Sounds easy, right? Well, not exactly. The first time you implement this, you may need to do it a lot. I'm talking twenty to thirty times or more on the first night. If you are consistent and bring your child back every time, this should improve pretty rapidly. But you need to be committed to doing this for a week. I also don't recommend it for children who are very anxious or fearful.

THE CAMPSITE METHOD

Another alternative, which works for many families, is setting up an alternative sleep space in your bedroom—like a little campsite. This can work well for anxious kids, helping reassure them and helping you get a better night's sleep.

The first step is to set up a sleeping bag and pillow in your room, out of the way (so you don't stumble over your child accidentally on the way to the bathroom in the middle of the night). Set it up in advance so everything your child needs is in place. I don't recommend setting up another bed, because you want this space to be less comfortable than her own bed.

Next, tell her that you have set up a place for her to camp out in your room at night if she gets worried or lonely. She can come into your room whenever she wants to. But here is the key: she can't come into your room and wake you or your partner up. Explain that you are very tired and you need her help getting a good night's sleep. She can stay in your room—as long as she does not disturb you. If she wakes you up at night, she will need to return to her room (à la the Silent Return, described in the previous section). *Follow through on this.*

If you prefer a softer touch, you can use a reward system, as described in Chapter 8. Offer your child rewards for spending the night in her own bed *or* for coming into your room without waking you up. Do not offer a reward if you are woken up at night.

THE DREADED EARLY MORNING AWAKENINGS

Early morning awakenings are painful. My younger son routinely woke up daily at 4:30 a.m. between six and eight months of age. This was not appreciated by his parents, to say the least. As I muddled through this, my sleep-deprived brain thought it would be good for me to lie down with him, but not in our bed, so we lay on the floor. I brought my pillow and blanket and pathetically lay down next to a cooing infant whose greatest joy was inserting his hands into my mouth as I tried to get an extra twenty minutes of sleep.

You need to be a bit realistic about the time that your child wakes up. Many children happily wake up between 5:30 and 6:30 a.m. *This is normal.* That does not make it any less painful, but you need to calibrate your expectations to the natural rhythms of your child's body. Most young kids are morning people. If your child is fired up for the day and happy and well rested through the afternoon, she may just need a little bit less sleep than her peers.

Some children, however, routinely wake up before dawn. This can be a problem, especially if they wake up irritable or tired, or if they are sleepier than they should be later in the day. This could be a sleep onset association, or a habit created by bringing your child into your bed with you every time she wakes up before dawn, or by handing your child an iPad every morning when she materializes at your bedside. Look at the reinforcement you are providing and eliminate it. Get up when your child gets up. Make it understood to older children that they may wake up early and read a book or play quietly. They should not be playing video games or watching TV until you deem it appropriate. (I would make an exception for the weekends—once my boys got older, we let them go downstairs and watch a show so we could get an extra thirty minutes of sleep.)

If you are still struggling, I like the Morning Light protocol, which was developed by none other than the sleep superstar Dr. Brett Kuhn. I've adapted it to use the light to provide a very nice sleep-time cue as well.

1. **Get a light source on a timer.** You can spring for one of these very nice OK to Wake! clocks, but I actually prefer a simple mechanical timer that you plug into an outlet and a nightlight of your child's choice. Note that you need a mechanical timer with fifteen-minute intervals, and a simple nightlight (one that does not have a light-sensing mode).

2. **Set the nightlight to go on thirty minutes prior to bedtime and to go off at the time that your child is currently waking up.** This provides another cue for him that it is time to go to sleep.

3. **At bedtime, point out that the light is on.** Say, "It's sleeping time."

4. **If your child wakes up during the night, point out that the nightlight is still on.** Say, "The light is still on. It's sleeping time."

5. **Set the light to go off at the time your child usually wakes up.** When the light goes on in the morning, go in and make a big deal: "The light is off! It's waking time!" Praise your child effusively. You can also couple this with a reward system if you like, but praise is usually enough. Note that if your child is still asleep, you don't need to wake him.

6. **After five days of this pattern, you can move the wake time later by fifteen minutes.** You can move the time later every three to five days until you get to a more reasonable hour. Note that you can't make your child sleep during that time (although he may); it is acceptable if he plays quietly in bed. I recommend a target wake time of 6:00–6:30 a.m.

A few other thoughts: First, consistency, as always, is fundamental. Make sure you respond to night wakings and early morning awakenings the same way. Second, don't let your child play with the timer. Third (and this is obvious), make sure that your child can see the light from his crib or bed.

Coda

I wrote this book so that your whole family can get a better night of sleep. I hope that I was successful, and that you learned how to hack your child's habits (and your own) to enable you to be better rested, happier, and healthier.

Parenting is a journey, and you are bound to take some unexpected detours. For example, I never thought during my pediatric residency that I would serve my picky son a plate of microwaved pepperoni for dinner out of desperation. Sometimes things aren't perfect. Give yourself a break. Take a deep breath and remember: you've got this.

I'D LOVE TO hear from you about what has worked for you and what hasn't. You can reach me pretty easily online.

Twitter: @drcanapari
Facebook: https://www.facebook.com/CraigCanapariMD
Instagram: drcanapari

The handouts and sleep diaries are available on my website at https://drcraigcanapari.com/nevertoolate.

REFERENCES

There are a few books that I highly recommend to the pediatric provider (or interested parent) who wants to delve more deeply. I have found them very useful in my practice and in the preparation of this book.

Kazdin, Alan. *The Kazdin Method for Parenting the Defiant Child.* New York: Houghton Mifflin Harcourt, 2008.

Meltzer, L. J., and V. McLaughlin Crabtree. *Pediatric Sleep Problems: A Clinician's Guide to Behavioral Interventions.* Washington, DC: American Psychological Association, 2015.

Mindell, J. A., and J. A. Owens. *A Clinical Guide to Pediatric Sleep.* 3rd ed. Philadelphia: Lippincott Williams & Wilkins, 2015.

Sheldon, S., R. Ferber, M. Kryger, and D. Gozal, eds. *Principles and Practice of Pediatric Sleep Medicine.* 2nd ed. London: Elsevier Saunders, 2014.

Following are specific references mentioned in the text.

INTRODUCTION

Badin, Emily, Cynthia Haddad, and Jess Parker Shatkin. "Insomnia: The Sleeping Giant of Pediatric Public Health." *Current Psychiatry Reports* 18, no. 5 (2016): 47. doi:10.1007/s11920-016-0687-0.

Duhigg, Charles. *The Power of Habit: Why We Do What We Do in Life and Business.* New York: Random House, 2012.

Green, Penelope. "Sleep Is the New Status Symbol." *New York Times*, April 8, 2017. https://www.nytimes.com/2017/04/08/fashion/sleep-tips-and-tools.html.

Kelly, Yvonne, John Kelly, and Amanda Sacker. "Time for Bed: Associations with Cognitive Performance in 7-Year-Old Children: A Longitudinal Population-Based Study." *Journal of Epidemiology and Community Health* 67, no. 11 (2013): 926–31. doi:10.1136/jech-2012-202024.

Williams, Kate E., Jan M. Nicholson, Sue Walker, and Donna Berthelsen. "Early Childhood Profiles of Sleep Problems and Self-Regulation Predict Later School Adjustment." *British Journal of Educational Psychology* 86, no. 2 (2016): 331–50. doi:10.1111/bjep.12109.

CHAPTER 1: THE BIOLOGY OF BEDTIME

Berry, R. B., R. Brooks, C. E. Gamaldo, S. M. Harding, R. M. Lloyd, C. L. Marcus, and B. V. Vaughn for the American Academy of Sleep Medicine. *The AASM Manual for the Scoring of Sleep and Associated Events: Rules, Terminology and Technical Specifications.* Version 2.2. Darien, IL: American Academy of Sleep Medicine, 2015.

Druckerman, Pamela. *Bringing Up Bébé: One American Mother Discovers the Wisdom of French Parenting.* New York: Penguin Books, 2014.

Hanson, Michele. "French Children Don't Throw Food by Pamela Druckerman—Review." *The Guardian.* January 20, 2012. http://www.theguardian.com/books/2012/jan/20/french-children-food-pamela-druckerman.

Henderson, J. M. T., K. G. France, J. L. Owens, and N. M. Blampied. "Sleeping Through the Night: The Consolidation of Self-Regulated Sleep Across the First Year of Life." *Pediatrics* 126, no. 5 (2010): e1081–87. doi:10.1542/peds.2010-0976.

Henderson, Jacqueline M. T., Karyn G. France, and Neville M. Blampied. "The Consolidation of Infants' Nocturnal Sleep Across the First Year of Life." *Sleep Medicine Reviews* 15, no. 4 (2011): 211–20. doi:10.1016/j.smrv.2010.08.003.

Hirshkowitz, Max, Kaitlyn Whiton, Steven M. Albert, Cathy Alessi, Oliviero Bruni, Lydia DonCarlos, Nancy Hazen, et al. "National Sleep Foundation's Updated Sleep Duration Recommendations: Final Report." *Sleep Health* 1, no. 4 (2015): 233–43. doi:10.1016/j.sleh.2015.10.004.

Kleitman, N. *Sleep and Wakefulness*. 2nd ed. Chicago: University of Chicago Press, 1963.

Kleitman, N., and T. G. Engelmann. "Sleep Characteristics of Infants." *Journal of Applied Physiology* 6, no. 5 (1953): 269–82. doi:10.1152/jappl.1953.6.5.269.

Paruthi, Shalini, Lee J. Brooks, Carolyn D'Ambrosio, Wendy A. Hall, Suresh Kotagal, Robin M. Lloyd, Beth A. Malow, et al. "Recommended Amount of Sleep for Pediatric Populations: A Consensus Statement of the American Academy of Sleep Medicine." *Journal of Clinical Sleep Medicine* 12 (2016): 785–86. doi:10.5664/jcsm.5866.

Task Force on Sudden Infant Death Syndrome. "SIDS and Other Sleep-Related Infant Deaths: Expansion of Recommendations for a Safe Infant Sleeping Environment." *Pediatrics* 128, no. 5 (2011): 1030–39. doi:10.1542/peds.2011-2284.

Touchette, Evelyne, Ginette Dionne, Nadine Forget-Dubois, Dominique Petit, Daniel Pérusse, Bruno Falissard, Richard E. Tremblay, Michel Boivin, and Jacques Y. Montplaisir. "Genetic and Environmental Influences on Daytime and Nighttime Sleep Duration in Early Childhood." *Pediatrics* 131, no. 6 (2013): e1874–80. doi:10.1542/peds.2012-2284.

CHAPTER 2: HACKING THE HABIT LOOP

Bloomfield, Elana R., and Jess P. Shatkin. "Parasomnias and Movement Disorders in Children and Adolescents." *Child and Adolescent*

Psychiatric Clinics of North America 18, no. 4 (2009): 947–65. doi:10.1016/j.chc.2009.04.010.

Davis, R, and J. Palca. "Where We Learn That Artificial Eyes Really Aren't Round at All." *Morning Edition*, NPR, August 11, 2014.

Duhigg, Charles. *The Power of Habit: Why We Do What We Do in Life and Business.* New York: Random House, 2012.

Dye, Thomas J., Sejal V. Jain, and Narong Simakajornboon. "Outcomes of Long-Term Iron Supplementation in Pediatric Restless Legs Syndrome/Periodic Limb Movement Disorder (RLS/PLMD)." *Sleep Medicine* 32 (April 2017): 213–19. doi:10.1016/j.sleep.2016.01.008.

Frank, N. C., A. Spirito, L. Stark, and J. Owens-Stively. "The Use of Scheduled Awakenings to Eliminate Childhood Sleepwalking." *Journal of Pediatric Psychology* 22, no. 3 (1997): 345–53.

Kaplan, K. "Single Moms Are the Most Sleep-Deprived People in America." *Los Angeles Times*, January 5, 2016.

Katz, Eliot S., and Carolyn M. D'Ambrosio. "Pediatric Obstructive Sleep Apnea Syndrome." *Clinics in Chest Medicine* 31, no. 2 (2010): 221–34. doi:10.1016/j.ccm.2010.02.002.

Kazdin, Alan. *The Kazdin Method for Parenting the Defiant Child.* New York: Houghton Mifflin Harcourt, 2008.

Lewandowski, Amy S., Teresa M. Ward, and Tonya M. Palermo. "Sleep Problems in Children and Adolescents with Common Medical Conditions." *Pediatric Clinics of North America* 58, no. 3 (2011): 699–713. https://doi.org/10.1016/j.pcl.2011.03.012.

Marche, S. "Why You Should Stop Yelling at Your Kids." *New York Times*, September 5, 2018.

Mindell, Jodi A., and Melisa Moore. "Bedtime Problems and Night Wakings." In *Principles and Practice of Pediatric Sleep Medicine*, 2nd ed., ed. S. Sheldon, R. Ferber, M. Kryger, and D. Gozal, 105–8. London: Elsevier Saunders, 2014.

Owens, J. A., A. Spirito, M. McGuinn, and C. Nobile. "Sleep Habits and Sleep Disturbance in Elementary School-Aged Children." *Journal of Developmental and Behavioral Pediatrics: JDBP* 21, no. 1 (2000): 27–36.

Shani Adir, Ayelet, Dganit Rozenman, Aharon Kessel, and Batya Engel-Yeger. "The Relationship Between Sensory Hypersensitivity and Sleep Quality of Children with Atopic Dermatitis." *Pediatric Dermatology* 26, no. 2 (2009): 143–49. doi:10.1111/j.1525-1470.2009.00904.x.

Werner, Helene, Peter Hunkeler, Caroline Benz, Luciano Molinari, Caroline Guyer, Fabienne Häfliger, Reto Huber, and Oskar G. Jenni. "The Zurich 3-Step Concept for the Management of Behavioral Sleep Disorders in Children: A Before-and-After Study." *Journal of Clinical Sleep Medicine* 11, no. 3 (2015): 241–49. doi:10.5664/jcsm.4536.

Wood, Wendy, and Dennis Rünger. "Psychology of Habit." *Annual Review of Psychology* 67 (2016): 289–314. doi:10.1146/annurev-psych-122414-033417.

CHAPTER 3: SMOOTHING THE PATH

Daniels, Elizabeth, Barbara Mandleco, and Karlen E. Luthy. "Assessment, Management, and Prevention of Childhood Temper Tantrums." *Journal of the American Academy of Nurse Practitioners* 24, no. 10 (2012): 569–73. doi:10.1111/j.1745-7599.2012.00755.x.

Doucleff, Michaeleen. "Is Sleeping with Your Baby as Dangerous as Doctors Say?" *Morning Edition*, NPR, May 21, 2018. https://www.npr.org/sections/goatsandsoda/2018/05/21/601289695/is-sleeping-with-your-baby-as-dangerous-as-doctors-say. Accessed June 1, 2018.

"The Effects of Excessive Crying." Ask Dr. Sears, https://www.askdrsears.com/topics/health-concerns/fussy-baby/science-excessive-crying-harmful. Accessed September 10, 2018.

Hiscock, Harriet, and Margot J. Davey. "Sleep Disorders in Infants and Children." *Journal of Paediatrics and Child Health* 54, no. 9 (2018): 941–44. doi:10.1111/jpc.12033.

Hysing, Mari, Allison G. Harvey, Leila Torgersen, Eivind Ystrom, Ted Reichborn-Kjennerud, and Borge Sivertsen. "Trajectories and Predictors of Nocturnal Awakenings and Sleep Duration in Infants." *Journal of Developmental and Behavioral Pediatrics* 35, no. 5 (2014): 309–16. doi:10.1097/DBP.0000000000000064.

Karen, R. "Becoming Attached." *Atlantic*, February 11, 1990.

Kluger, J. "The Science Behind Dr. Sears: Does It Stand Up?" *Time*, May 10, 2012.

Paul, I. M., E. E. Hohman, E. Loken, et al. "Mother-Infant Room-Sharing and Sleep Outcomes in the INSIGHT Study." *Pediatrics* 140, no. 1 (2017): e20170122. doi:10.1542/peds.2017-0122.

Task Force on Sudden Infant Death Syndrome. "SIDS and Other Sleep-Related Infant Deaths: Expansion of Recommendations for a Safe Infant Sleeping Environment." *Pediatrics* 128, no. 5 (2011): 1030–39. doi:10.1542/peds.2011-2284.

Teti, D. M. "Long-Term Co-sleeping with Baby Can Be a Sign of Family Problems." *Child and Family Blog*, June 1, 2016. https://www.childandfamilyblog.com/uncategorised/long-term-co-sleeping-baby-can-sign-family-problems.

Teti, Douglas M., Mina Shimizu, Brian Crosby, and Bo-Ram Kim. "Sleep Arrangements, Parent-Infant Sleep During the First Year, and Family Functioning." *Developmental Psychology* 52, no. 8 (2016): 1169–81. doi:10.1037/dev0000148.

CHAPTER 4: LOCATION, LOCATION, LOCATION

Canapari, C. A. "Is Your Sound Machine Harming Your Child's Hearing?" May 9, 2014. https://drcraigcanapari.com/is-your-sound-machine-harming-your-childs-hearing.

Carter, Ben, Philippa Rees, Lauren Hale, Darsharna Bhattacharjee, and Mandar S. Paradkar. "Association Between Portable Screen-Based Media Device Access or Use and Sleep Outcomes: A Systematic Review and Meta-Analysis." *JAMA Pediatrics* 170, no. 12 (2016): 1202–8. doi:10.1001/jamapediatrics.2016.2341.

Coffman, Mary F., and D. C. Dusevitch. *Uncle Lightfoot, Flip That Switch*. Pace, FL: Footpath Press, 2014.

Dennison, Barbara A., Tara A. Erb, and Paul L. Jenkins. "Television Viewing and Television in Bedroom Associated with Overweight Risk Among Low-Income Preschool Children." *Pediatrics* 109, no. 6 (2002): 1028–35.

Hugh, S. C., N. E. Wolter, E. J. Propst, and K. A. Gordon. "Infant Sleep Machines and Hazardous Sound Pressure Levels." *Pediatrics* 133, no. 4 (2014): 677–81. doi:10.1542/peds.2013-3617.

Johnson, Jeffrey G., Patricia Cohen, Stephanie Kasen, Michael B. First, and Judith S. Brook. "Association Between Television Viewing and Sleep Problems During Adolescence and Early Adulthood." *Archives of Pediatrics and Adolescent Medicine* 158, no. 6 (2004): 562–68. doi:10.1001/archpedi.158.6.562.

Kabali, Hilda K., Matilde M. Irigoyen, Rosemary Nunez-Davis, Jennifer G. Budacki, Sweta H. Mohanty, Kristin P. Leister, and Robert L. Bonner. "Exposure and Use of Mobile Media Devices by Young Children." *Pediatrics* 136, no. 6 (2015): 1044–50. doi:10.1542/peds.2015-2151.

Kushnir, Jonathan, and Avi Sadeh. "Assessment of Brief Interventions for Nighttime Fears in Preschool Children." *European Journal of Pediatrics* 171, no. 1 (2012): 67–75. https://doi.org/10.1007/s00431-011-1488-4.

Kushnir, Jonathan, and Avi Sadeh. "Sleep of Preschool Children with Night-Time Fears." *Sleep Medicine* 12, no. 9 (2011): 870–74. doi:10.1016/j.sleep.2011.03.022.

Meltzer, L. J., and V. McLaughlin Crabtree. "Nighttime Fears, Anxiety, and Recurrent Nightmares." In *Pediatric Sleep Problems: A Clinician's Guide to Behavioral Interventions.* Washington, DC: American Psychological Association, 2015.

Owens, J., R. Maxim, M. McGuinn, C. Nobile, M. Msall, and A. Alario. "Television-Viewing Habits and Sleep Disturbance in School Children." *Pediatrics* 104, no. 3 (1999): e27.

Sadeh, Avi, Shai Hen-Gal, and Liat Tikotzky. "Young Children's Reactions to War-Related Stress: A Survey and Assessment of an Innovative Intervention." *Pediatrics* 121, no. 1 (2008): 46–53. doi:10.1542/peds.2007-1348.

Tauman, R., H. Avni, A. Drori-Asayag, H. Nehama, M. Greenfeld, and Y. Leitner. "Sensory Profile in Infants and Toddlers with Behavioral

Insomnia and/or Feeding Disorders." *Sleep Medicine* 32 (April 2017): 83–86. doi:10.1016/j.sleep.2016.12.009.

CHAPTER 5: TIMING

Borbely, A. A. "A Two Process Model of Sleep Regulation." *Human Neurobiology* 1, no. 3 (1982): 195–204.

Bruni, Oliviero, Daniel Alonso-Alconada, Frank Besag, Valerie Biran, Wiebe Braam, Samuele Cortese, Romina Moavero, et al. "Current Role of Melatonin in Pediatric Neurology: Clinical Recommendations." *European Journal of Paediatric Neurology* 19, no. 2 (2015): 122–33. doi:10.1016/j.ejpn.2014.12.007.

Erland, Lauren A. E., and Praveen K. Saxena. "Melatonin Natural Health Products and Supplements: Presence of Serotonin and Significant Variability of Melatonin Content." *Journal of Clinical Sleep Medicine* 13, no. 2 (2017): 275–81. doi:10.5664/jcsm.6462.

Hirshkowitz, Max, Kaitlyn Whiton, Steven M. Albert, Cathy Alessi, Oliviero Bruni, Lydia DonCarlos, Nancy Hazen, et al. "National Sleep Foundation's Updated Sleep Duration Recommendations: Final Report." *Sleep Health* 1, no. 4 (2015): 233–43. doi:10.1016/j.sleh.2015.10.004.

Kelly, Yvonne, John Kelly, and Amanda Sacker. "Time for Bed: Associations with Cognitive Performance in 7-Year-Old Children: A Longitudinal Population-Based Study." *Journal of Epidemiology and Community Health* 67, no. 11 (2013): 926–31. doi:10.1136/jech-2012-202024.

Lavie, P. "Ultrashort Sleep-Waking Schedule. III. 'Gates' and 'Forbidden Zones' for Sleep." *Electroencephalography and Clinical Neurophysiology* 63, no. 5 (1986): 414–25.

LeBourgeois, Monique K., Kenneth P. Wright, Hannah B. LeBourgeois, and Oskar G. Jenni. "Dissonance Between Parent-Selected Bedtimes and Young Children's Circadian Physiology Influences Nighttime Settling Difficulties." *Mind, Brain and Education* 7, no. 4 (2013): 234–42. doi:10.1111/mbe.12032.

Paruthi, Shalini, Lee J. Brooks, Carolyn D'Ambrosio, Wendy A. Hall, Suresh Kotagal, Robin M. Lloyd, Beth A. Malow, et al. "Recommended

Amount of Sleep for Pediatric Populations: A Consensus Statement of the American Academy of Sleep Medicine." *Journal of Clinical Sleep Medicine* 12 (2016): 785–86. doi:10.5664/jcsm.5866.

Zee, P. C., and F. W. Turek. "Introduction: Master Circadian Clock and Master Circadian Rhythm" In *Principles and Practice of Sleep Medicine*, 6th ed., ed. M. Kryger, T. Roth, and W. C. Dement, 340–33. Philadelphia: Elsevier, 2017.

CHAPTER 6: BEDTIME FLOW

Hale, Lauren, Lawrence M. Berger, Monique K. LeBourgeois, and Jeanne Brooks-Gunn. "A Longitudinal Study of Preschoolers' Language-Based Bedtime Routines, Sleep Duration, and Well-Being." *Journal of Family Psychology* 25, no. 3 (2011): 423–33. doi:10.1037/a0023564.

Katz, Terry, and Beth Malow. *Solving Sleep Problems in Children with Autism Spectrum Disorders: A Guide for Frazzled Families*. Bethesda, MD: Woodbine House, 2014.

Kitsaras, George, Michaela Goodwin, Julia Allan, Michael P. Kelly, and Iain A. Pretty. "Bedtime Routines, Child Wellbeing & Development." *BMC Public Health* 18, no. 1 (2018): 386. doi:10.1186/s12889-018-5290-3.

Mindell, Jodi A., Lorena S. Telofski, Benjamin Wiegand, and Ellen S. Kurtz. "A Nightly Bedtime Routine: Impact on Sleep in Young Children and Maternal Mood." *Sleep* 32, no. 5 (2009): 599–606.

Meltzer, L. J., and V. McLaughlin Crabtree. "Bedtime Stalling, Protests, and Curtain Calls," in *Pediatric Sleep Problems: A Clinician's Guide to Behavioral Interventions*. Washington, DC: American Psychological Association, 2015.

Sexton, Sumi M., and Ruby Natale. "Risks and Benefits of Pacifiers." *American Family Physician* 79, no. 8 (2009): 681–85.

CHAPTER 7: THE SOLUTION BEGINS WITH YOU

Callahan, Alice Green. *The Science of Mom*. Baltimore, MD: Johns Hopkins University Press, 2015.

Meltzer, Lisa J., and Jodi A. Mindell. "Systematic Review and Meta-Analysis of Behavioral Interventions for Pediatric Insomnia." *Journal of Pediatric Psychology* 39, no. 8 (2014): 932–48. https://doi.org/10.1093/jpepsy/jsu041.

Mindell, J. A., B. Kuhn, D. S. Lewin, L. J. Meltzer, and A. Sadeh for the American Academy of Sleep Medicine. "Behavioral Treatment of Bedtime Problems and Night Wakings in Infants and Young Children." *Sleep* 29, no. 10 (2006): 1263–76.

Morgenthaler, Timothy I., Judith Owens, Cathy Alessi, Brian Boehlecke, Terry M. Brown, Jack Coleman, Leah Friedman, et al. "Practice Parameters for Behavioral Treatment of Bedtime Problems and Night Wakings in Infants and Young Children." *Sleep* 29, no. 10 (2006): 1277–81.

Price, A. M. H., M. Wake, O. C. Ukoumunne, and H. Hiscock. "Five-Year Follow-up of Harms and Benefits of Behavioral Infant Sleep Intervention: Randomized Trial." *Pediatrics* 130, no. 4 (2012): 643–51. doi:10.1542/peds.2011-3467.

CHAPTER 8: CHOOSING YOUR CONSEQUENCES

Angier, N. "A Baby Wails, and the Adult World Comes Running." *New York Times*, September 4, 2017.

Ashbaugh, R., and S. M. Peck. "Treatment of Sleep Problems in a Toddler: A Replication of the Faded Bedtime with Response Cost Protocol." *Journal of Applied Behavior Analysis* 31, no. 1 (1998): 127–29. https://doi.org/10.1901/jaba.1998.31-127.

Blunden, Sarah. "Behavioural Treatments to Encourage Solo Sleeping in Pre-School Children: An Alternative to Controlled Crying." *Journal of Child Health Care: For Professionals Working with Children in the Hospital and Community* 15, no. 2 (2011): 107–17. https://doi.org/10.1177/1367493510397623.

Freeman, Kurt A. "Treating Bed Time Resistance with the Bed Time Pass: A Systematic Replication and Component Analysis with 3-Year-Olds." *Journal of Applied Behavior Analysis* 39, no. 4 (2006): 423–28.

Friman, P. C., K. E. Hoff, C. Schnoes, K. A. Freeman, D. W. Woods, and N. Blum. "The Bedtime Pass: An Approach to Bedtime Crying and Leaving the Room." *Archives of Pediatrics & Adolescent Medicine* 153, no. 10 (1999): 1027–29.

Honaker, Sarah Morsbach, and Lisa J. Meltzer. "Bedtime Problems and Night Wakings in Young Children: An Update of the Evidence." *Paediatric Respiratory Reviews* 15, no. 4 (2014): 333–39. https://doi.org/10.1016/j.prrv.2014.04.011.

Katz, Terry, and Beth Malow. *Solving Sleep Problems in Children with Autism Spectrum Disorders: A Guide for Frazzled Families.* Bethesda, MD: Woodbine House, 2014.

Kazdin, Alan. *The Kazdin Method for Parenting the Defiant Child.* New York: Houghton Mifflin Harcourt, 2008.

Kuhn, Brett, ed. "Part III: BSM Protocols for Pediatric Sleep Disorders." In *Behavioral Treatments for Sleep Disorders*, ed. Michael Perlis, Mark Aloia, and Brett Kuhn. Burlington, MA: Academic Press, 2011.

Meltzer, L. J., and V. McLaughlin Crabtree, V. *Pediatric Sleep Problems: A Clinician's Guide to Behavioral Interventions.* Washington, DC: American Psychological Association, 2015.

Moore, Brie A., Patrick C. Friman, Alan E. Fruzzetti, and Ken MacAleese. "Brief Report: Evaluating the Bedtime Pass Program for Child Resistance to Bedtime—a Randomized, Controlled Trial." *Journal of Pediatric Psychology* 32, no. 3 (2007): 283–87. https://doi.org/10.1093/jpepsy/jsl025.

Paine, Sarah, and Michael Gradisar. "A Randomised Controlled Trial of Cognitive-Behaviour Therapy for Behavioural Insomnia of Childhood in School-Aged Children." *Behaviour Research and Therapy* 49, no. 6–7 (2011): 379–88. https://doi.org/10.1016/j.brat.2011.03.008.

Piazza, C. C., and W. Fisher. "A Faded Bedtime with Response Cost Protocol for Treatment of Multiple Sleep Problems in Children." *Journal of Applied Behavior Analysis* 24, no. 1 (1991): 129–40. https://doi.org/10.1901/jaba.1991.24-129.

CHAPTER 9: STAYING IN THE (HABIT) LOOP

Anderson, L. "A Sleep Regression Isn't a Setback, It's a Sign." *Lifehacker*, November 30, 2017. https://offspring.lifehacker.com/a-sleep-regression-isnt-a-setback-its-a-sign-1820799094.

Kuhn, Brett R. "Practical Strategies for Managing Behavioral Sleep Problems in Young Children." *Clinics in Sleep Medicine* 9, no. 2 (2014): 181–97. doi:10.1016/j.jsmc.2014.03.004.

Lindeman, R. "There is No Such Thing as a Sleep Regression!" *Sleep, Baby*, February 13, 2016, www.essentiallyhealthychild.com/2016/02/13/there-is-no-such-thing-sleep-regression.

Thorpe, K., S. Staton, E. Sawyer, C. Pattinson, C. Haden, and S. Smith. "Napping, Development and Health from 0 to 5 Years: A Systematic Review." *Archives of Disease in Childhood* 100, no. 7 (2015): 615–22. doi:10.1136/archdischild-2014-307241.

Weissbluth, M. *Healthy Sleep Habits, Happy Child*. 3rd ed. New York: Ballantine, 2003.

ACKNOWLEDGMENTS

MANY PEOPLE HAVE helped me as I have written this book. It all began in 2016, when Annie Murphy Paul introduced me to my agent, Alison Mackeen at Sterling Lord Literistic, who was willing to sit down with a first-time author and guide me through the process of writing a book proposal. Alison's fingerprints are all over this book, both in elegant turns of phrase and in the overall structure of the book. Thanks also to Lizzie Skurnick, who gave me a parent's-eye view of the proposal.

Alison and her assistant, Jenny Stephens, found this book a great home at Rodale/Penguin Random House, where Marisa Vigilante got me started and my editor Alyse Diamond got me across the finish line with panache. Along the way, Andrea Thompson provided invaluable editing, helping me to shape the manuscript as it grew, and kept me on track.

I've abused the generosity of my good friends who have read the proposal and then the book on fairly short notice and helped me through various bouts with nerves along the way. Thanks to Dr. Julian Davies and Dr. Monica Ordway for their insights, and also the fact that they laugh at my jokes.

No one makes it very far in medicine (or life) without good mentors. I have been blessed with many, including Drs. Judy Owens, Meir Kryger, Bernard Kinane, and Alia Bazzy-Asaad. Thanks to Dr. Wendy Sue Swanson, aka "Seattle Mama Doc," who let me write my first sleep articles for parents on her site, as well as Dr. Natasha Burgert and many of my other pediatrician blogger friends.

My colleagues and the staff at Yale, both in the Pediatric Respiratory Division and the Pediatric Sleep Center, were tremendously understanding when it came to crunch time for structuring, researching, and writing this book. Special thanks to Chris Bailey, who skillfully runs the Sleep Center.

I've learned so much from my colleagues and predecessors in the field of pediatric sleep medicine. Many of the ideas in this book are built upon the work of others, and I have tried to give credit to any and all whose research, knowledge, and experience have shaped my approach to sleep problems in children.

I also want to thank my family: my parents, Carolyn and "Diamond" Dave Canapari; my baby brother, Matt (who narrowly missed having an embarrassing anecdote about his difficulty pooping as a child relayed in the book), and his wife, Sarah; my sisters- and brothers-in-law, Crissy, Jeremy, Laura, and Rob; my nieces and nephews, Julia, Ryan, Andrew, and Zoe; and the rest of the extended Canapari/Lucci/Schnabl clan.

Finally, thanks to my wife, Jeanna, whose tireless love and support is the bedrock of my life, and to our beautiful boys, who fill each day with joy and adventure. I'm grateful to them both for being good sleepers (people ask me all the time if they are) and for being the best little dudes around.

INDEX